# TED & JOE

## PLAYERS' MEMORIES OF TWO ICONS

# TED & JOE

## PLAYERS' MEMORIES OF TWO ICONS

BY JOHN VALERINO

INTRODUCTION BY YOGI BERRA

Copyright © 2010 by MACKQUINN, LLC.

All rights reserved. No part of this book may be reproduced, stored in a retrieval system or transmitted by any means, electronic, mechanical, photocopying, recording or otherwise without written permission from:

MACKQUINN, LLC
P.O. Box 7896, Lakeland, Florida 33807
MACKQUINNLLC@aol.com

Printed in the United States of America
ISBN: 978-1-59571-514-2
Library of Congress Control Number: 2010923128

Word Association Publishers
205 Fifth Avenue
Tarentum, PA. 15084
www.wordassociation.com
1-800-827-7903

Book Design: Gina Datres, Word Association Publishers

## DEDICATION

This book is dedicated to my late parents, Betty (1920-98) and Michael (1919-2006) Valerino, who gave me every opportunity to play athletics and visit many major league ballparks after I became a fan of the game in 1958 at the age of 6, and for not throwing out my baseball card collection when I went off to college.

# TABLE OF CONTENTS

| | |
|---|---|
| Acknowledgments | 1 |
| Introduction by Yogi Berra | 5 |
| CHAPTER 1: Joe DiMaggio up close | 9 |
| CHAPTER 2: Ted Williams up close | 17 |
| CHAPTER 3: DiMaggio's streak ends at 56 in Cleveland | 25 |
| CHAPTER 4: Williams chases .400 on the final day | 49 |
| CHAPTER 5: Teammates and rivals remember Ted & Joe | 67 |
| CHAPTER 6: DiMaggio finally enters the Hall of Fame | 153 |
| CHAPTER 7: Williams gets the call from the Hall | 159 |
| CHAPTER 8: The DiMaggio-Williams feud in 1949 | 167 |
| CHAPTER 9: Ted & Joe said it | 173 |
| CHAPTER 10: Ted & Joe by the numbers | 177 |
| About the Author | 193 |

## ACKNOWLEDGMENTS

The author would like to thank the following players for their participation and cooperation in the completion of this book:

**YOGI BERRA,** Yankees (1946-63); Mets (1965)

**DOM DIMAGGIO,** Red Sox (1940-42; 1946-53)

**BOBBY DOERR,** Red Sox (1937-44; 1946-51)

**BOB FELLER,** Indians (1936-41; 1945-56)

**WHITEY FORD,** Yankees (1950; 1953-67)

**DON GUTTERIDGE,** Cardinals (1936-40); Browns (1942-45); Red Sox (1946-47); Pirates (1948)

**RALPH HOUK,** Yankees (1947-54)

**SID HUDSON,** Senators (1940-42; 1946-52); Red Sox (1952-54)

**GEORGE KELL,** Athletics (1943-46); Tigers (1946-52); Red Sox (1952-54); White Sox (1954-56); Orioles (1956-57).

**LES MCCRABB,** Athletics (1939-42; 1950)

**JOHN MOSS,** Browns (1946-50); Red Sox (1951); Browns (1951-53); Orioles (1954-55); White Sox (1955-58)

**JOHNNY PESKY,** Red Sox (1942; 1946-52); Tigers (1952-54); Senators (1954)

**BILLY PIERCE,** Tigers (1945, 1948); White Sox (1949-61); Giants (1962-64)

**EDDIE ROBINSON,** Indians (1942, 1946-48); Senators (1949-50); White Sox (1950-52); Athletics (1953); Yankees (1954-56); Athletics (1956); Tigers, Indians and Orioles (1957)

**AL ROSEN,** Indians (1947-56)

**CARL SCHEIB,** Athletics (1943-45; 1947-54); Cardinals (1954)

**BOBBY SHANTZ,** Athletics (1949-56); Yankees (1957-60); Pirates (1961); Astros (1962); Cardinals (1962-64); Cubs (1964); Phillies (1964)

**ROY SIEVERS,** Browns (1949-53); Senators (1954-59); White Sox (1960-61); Phillies (1962-64); Senators (1965)

**VIRGIL TRUCKS,** Tigers (1941-43; 1945-52); Browns (1953); White Sox (1953-55); Tigers (1956); Athletics (1957-58); Yankees (1958)

**MICKEY VERNON,** Senators (1939-43; 1946-48); Indians (1949-50); Senators (1950-55); Red Sox (1956-57); Indians (1958); Braves (1959); Pirates (1960)

## SOURCES

Baseball-Almanac.com

BaseballLibrary.com

Baseball-Reference.com

Boston Globe

Boston Red Sox

Chicago White Sox

Cleveland Indians

Cleveland Plain Dealer

"Hitter: The Life and Turmoils of Ted Williams," by Ed Linn (Harcourt Brace & Co., 1993)

"Joe DiMaggio: An Informal Biography," by George De Gregorio (Stein & Day Publishers, 1983)

"Joe DiMaggio: The Hero's Life," by Richard Ben Cramer (Simon & Schuster, 2001)

"Joltin' Joe DiMaggio," by Allan Selig (Da Capo Press, 1999)

MajorLeagueBaseball.com

National Baseball Hall of Fame

New York Times

New York Yankees

"Ted Williams: The Biography of an American Hero," by Leigh Montville (Anchor Publishing, 2005)

"What Do You Think of Ted Williams Now?: A Remembrance," by Richard Ben Cramer (Simon & Schuster, 2002)

Wikipedia Encyclopedia

## PHOTO CREDITS

**NATIONAL BASEBALL HALL OF FAME:**

Joe DiMaggio (chapter 1, page 8)

Ken Keltner (chapter 3, page 25)

National Baseball Hall of Fame logo (chapter 7, page 159)

**MICHAEL F. VALERINO COLLECTION:**

all remaining photos

**SPECIAL THANKS TO:**

Dr. Robin Wooten

Dr. Thomas McClane

# INTRODUCTION

## BY YOGI BERRA

HALL OF FAMER & TEN-TIME
WORLD CHAMPION WITH THE YANKEES

People always ask me to compare Ted Williams and Joe DiMaggio. I don't like comparing anybody to anybody, because I don't. When I'm asked to compare eras, or if I'd rather play in our day rather than today with the big money and smaller ballparks, what does it matter? We had fun, worked hard and loved the game. So did Ted and Joe.

*Continued next page*

Ted was one heck of a hitter and a good man. Loyal and generous and a real hard out. He studied hitting like nobody else. And he loved talking hitting to anybody. It's hard to believe he gave up five prime years for the service and was still extraordinarily so good. Give him credit, he became what he always pledged to become, the greatest hitter ever.

If anyone thought Ted was jealous of Joe, I think they're wrong. Ted had a good appreciation and respect for him. Remember, he was a great friend and teammate of Dom DiMaggio, Joe's brother. As far as I know, Ted and Joe always got along good and were friendly even if they were rivals. And we had a darn good rivalry with the Red Sox in those days, too.

Ted and I always got along great. For years we served on the Hall of Fame Veterans Committee together. He had a great sense of justice and fairness and everyone had true respect for his opinions.

What can I say about DiMag? I played with him for five years and he was great—the best overall player I ever played with. I never saw him make a mistake. He did everything perfect. He was quiet, a little aloof and sometimes misunderstood. All I know is he was great to me and always played cards with us on the train. He took enormous pride in being a Yankee and set a good example the way he played and hustled and prepared. He was a model ballplayer.

Of course, there's no telling what Joe would've done if he

played his career in Boston's Fenway Park. As a right-handed hitter, he might have lost 200 home runs playing in Yankee Stadium. Who knows? But he never complained. To him, winning mattered the most.

Ted was Ted and Joe was Joe. I'm proud they're both represented in our Museum & Learning Center at Montclair (N.J.) State University. Both were true legends and they don't come any better.

> "WHAT CAN I SAY ABOUT DiMAG? I PLAYED WITH HIM FOR FIVE YEARS AND HE WAS GREAT - THE BEST OVERALL PLAYER I EVER PLAYED WITH."

Personality and style-wise, they were different. For one thing, Joe was an elegant dresser, wore tailored blue suits. And Ted always went against the grain. I don't think he owned a tie. Even at his Hall of Fame induction, when he went in with Casey Stengel, Ted wore a golf shirt.

If you want to know more, read on. John Valerino has pitched a perfect game talking to players who knew them best — guys like Dom DiMaggio, Whitey Ford, George Kell, Bob Feller, Bobby Doerr, Johnny Pesky, Ralph Houk, Al Rosen and Mickey Vernon. I was lucky to know both Ted and Joe, two of the best ever. This book is the next-best-thing to knowing them, too.

Joe DiMaggio the rookie in 1936

# CHAPTER 1
# Joe DiMaggio Up Close

| | |
|---|---|
| **FULL NAME:** | Joseph Paul DiMaggio Jr. (born Giuseppe Paolo DiMaggio). |
| **NICKNAMES:** | Joltin' Joe, The Yankee Clipper. |
| **BORN:** | Nov. 25, 1914, Martinez, CA. |
| **PARENTS:** | "Giuseppe" was for his father, "Paolo" for St. Paul, his father's favorite Saint. Joe was the fourth son and the eighth child born to Giuseppe and Rosalie DiMaggio. Joe's two older brothers, Tom and Michael, joined the family fishing business. His two other brothers, Dominic and Vince, joined Joe on the sandlots because they claimed the smell of fish made them sick. Their father considered it pure cases of laziness. |
| **DIED:** | March 8, 1999, Hollywood, FL. (lung cancer). He is buried in Colma, CA |
| **BATTED/THREW:** | Right/right |
| **HEIGHT/WEIGHT:** | 6-feet-2, 193 pounds |
| **ML SEASONS:** | 13 (1936-42, Yankees; 1946-51, Yankees) |
| **ML DEBUT:** | May 3, 1936 (Yankees 14, Browns 5) |

| | |
|---|---|
| **CAREER GAMES:** | 1,736 |
| **FINAL ML GAME:** | Oct. 10, 1951 (World Series Game 6: Yanks 4, Giants 3) |
| **POSITION:** | Center field |
| **CAREER AT-BATS:** | 6,821 |
| **CAREER HITS:** | 2,214 |
| **CAREER RUNS:** | 1,390 |
| **CAREER DOUBLES:** | 389 |
| **CAREER TRIPLES:** | 131 |
| **CAREER BASE-ON-BALLS:** | 790 |
| **CAREER STRIKEOUTS:** | 369 |
| **CAREER HOME RUNS:** | 361 |
| **CAREER RBIS:** | 1,537 |
| **CAREER BATTING AVG.:** | .325 |
| **CAREER FIELDING PCT.:** | .978 |
| **CAREER PUTOUTS:** | 4,529 |
| **CAREER ASSISTS:** | 153 |
| **CAREER ERRORS:** | 105 |
| **BATTING CHAMPIONSHIPS:** | 2 (1939 - .381), (1940 - .352) |

| | |
|---|---|
| **MVP:** | **1939** (.381 avg., 108 runs, 30 homers, 126 RBIs)<br>**1941** (.357 avg., 122 runs, 30 homers, 125 RBIs)<br>**1947** (.315 avg., 97 runs, 20 homers, 97 RBIs) |
| **ML PLAYER OF THE YEAR:** | 1939 |
| **ALL-STAR SELECTIONS:** | 13 (did not play in 1946 and 1951 due to injuries) |
| **ALL-STAR BATTING STATS:** | .225 average (9-for-40, 7 runs, 1 homer, 6 RBIs) |
| **ALL-STAR HIGHLIGHT:** | Batting fourth behind brother Dom, George Kell and Ted Williams, DiMaggio went 2-for-4, doubled and drove in 3 runs to lead the American League to an 11-7 victory in the 1949 game at Ebbetts Field. |
| **TRIPLE CROWNS:** | None |
| **WORLD SERIES RECORD:** | 9-1 (beat the Giants in 1936, 1937, 1951; beat the Dodgers in 1941, 1947, 1949; beat the Cubs in 1938, the Reds in 1939 and the Phillies in 1950; lost to the Cardinals in five games in 1942) |
| **WORLD SERIES BATTING AVG:** | .271 (54-for-199, 27 runs, 30 RBIs, 8 homers) |

**HOW HE BECAME A YANKEE:** On Nov. 21, 1934, the San Francisco Seals of the Pacific Coast League sent DiMaggio to the Yankees for seldom-used Doc Farrell, Floyd Newkirk, Jim Densmore, Ted Norbet and $5,000.

**DIMAGGIO THE EXECUTIVE:** Vice-President of the Baltimore Orioles (1979 - 1988); Executive Vice-President and batting instructor for the Oakland A's (1968 - 1969); official television spokesman for "Mr. Coffee."

**MARRIAGES:** Joe married actress Dorothy Arnold (15 films) in 1939 and had one child, Joseph III, who was born in 1941. The couple divorced after five years. In 1954, Joe married actress Marilyn Monroe after the two met on an arranged dinner date. The media called it "The Marriage of the Century." The marriage lasted less than a year, though. Joe was retired and wanted to settle down, while Monroe's movie career was reaching its peak. The two remained close friends until Monroe's death in August 1962, the result of an overdose of sleeping pills. Joe, who never married again, took charge of the funeral. He barred President John Kennedy and his brother, Attorney General Bobby, from the funeral, believing they played a role in Monroe's untimely death. Prior to her death, it was rumored that the two were planning to remarry. Several reports stated the two were planning to make the announcement three days prior to her death. For the next 20 years, he had a dozen roses placed at her crypt three times a week.

**MILITARY SERVICE:** DiMaggio enlisted in the U.S. Army on Feb. 17, 1942. He was stationed in Santa Ana, CA., Atlantic City and Hawaii during his 31-month stint. A sergeant, he served as a physical education teacher and played baseball.

**FAVORITE QUOTE:** "There is always some kid who may be seeing me for the first or last time. I owe him my best."

**FAST FACT:** DiMaggio took great pleasure in the building of a children's wing in 1992 called the Joe DiMaggio Children's Hospital at Memorial Regional Hospital in Hollywood, FL. "Whether rich or poor, no child is turned away," he said. His legacy has raised millions of dollars for the hospital.

**DID YOU KNOW?** DiMaggio appeared in the original motion picture *Angels in the Outfield* in 1951, as well as *The First of May* (released in 1999). According to the film's director,

Paul Sirmons, DiMaggio refused payment because the movie's subject, foster children, was dear to him, but Screen Actors Guild rules mandated he take the minimum $250 per day fee.

**HALL OF FAME:** Class of 1955

Joe and his second wife, movie glamour girl Marilyn Monroe, who he married in 1954. The marriage lasted less than a year.

Ted Williams the rookie in 1939

# CHAPTER 2
# Ted Williams Up Close

| | |
|---|---|
| **FULL NAME:** | Theodore Samuel Williams. |
| **NICKNAMES:** | The Splendid Splinter, The Kid, The Thumper, Teddy Ballgame |
| **BORN:** | Aug. 30, 1918, San Diego, CA |
| **PARENTS:** | Williams was named after his father, Samuel Stuart Williams, and President Teddy Roosevelt. His father was a soldier, sheriff and photographer. His mother, May Venzor, was a Salvation Army worker. |
| **DIED:** | July 5, 2002, Inverness, FL. (heart failure). Although his daughter, Barbara Joyce Ferrell, produced a will stating Williams wished to be cremated, son John-Henry Williams produced a questionable document on an oil-stained napkin which stated his father wanted his body flown to the Alcor Life Extension Foundation in Scottsdale, AZ., where he was placed into cryonic suspension. |
| **BATTED/THREW:** | Left/right |
| **HEIGHT/WEIGHT:** | 6-feet-3, 205 pounds |

| | |
|---|---|
| **ML SEASONS:** | 19 (1939-42, Red Sox; 1946-60, Red Sox) |
| **ML DEBUT:** | April 20, 1939 (Yankees 2, Red Sox 0) |
| **CAREER GAMES:** | 2,292 |
| **FINAL ML GAME:** | Sept. 28, 1960 (Williams' home run against Jack Fisher in the eighth inning in his final at-bat propelled the Red Sox to a 5-4 win over the Orioles at Fenway Park). |
| **POSITION:** | Left field |
| **CAREER AT-BATS:** | 7,706 |
| **CAREER HITS:** | 2,654 |
| **CAREER RUNS:** | 1,798 |
| **CAREER DOUBLES:** | 525 |
| **CAREER TRIPLES:** | 71 |
| **CAREER BASE-ON-BALLS:** | 2,021 |
| **CAREER STRIKEOUTS:** | 709 |
| **CAREER RBIS:** | 1,839 |
| **CAREER HOME RUNS:** | 521 |
| **CAREER BATTING AVG.:** | .344 |
| **CAREER FIELDING PCT.:** | .974 |
| **CAREER PUTOUTS:** | 4,158 |
| **CAREER ASSISTS:** | 142 |

| | |
|---|---|
| **CAREER ERRORS:** | 113 |
| **BATTING TITLES:** | 6 (**1941** - .406), (**1942** - .356), (**1947** - .343), (**1948** - .369), (**1957** - .388), (**1958** - .328) |
| **MVP:** | **1946** (.342 average, 142 runs, 38 homers, 123 RBIs)<br>**1949** (.343, 150 runs, 43 homers, 159 RBIs) |
| **ML PLAYER/YEAR:** | 1941, 1942, 1947, 1949, 1957 |
| **ALL-STAR SELECTIONS:** | 21 (in 1959 and 1960, two All-Star Games were played) |
| **ALL-STAR BATTING STATS:** | .304 average (14-for-46, 10 runs, 4 homers, 12 RBIs) |
| **ALL-STAR HIGHLIGHT:** | Williams' two-out, bottom-of-the-ninth, upper-deck three-run homer to right field lifted the American League to a dramatic 6-5 come-from-behind victory over the National Leaguers in 1941. |
| **TRIPLE CROWNS:** | **1942** (.356, 141 runs, 36 homers, 137 RBIs)<br>**1947** (.343, 125 runs, 32 homers, 114 RBIs) |
| **WORLD SERIES RECORD:** | 0-1 (lost to the Cardinals in seven games in 1946) |
| **WORLD SERIES BATTING AVG.:** | .200 (no homers, 1 RBI) |

**HOW HE BECAME A RED SOX:** Former Athletics and White Sox second baseman Eddie Collins traveled to San Diego of the Pacific Coast League to sign a young second baseman by the name of Bobby Doerr (Hall of Fame Class of 1986). While he was there, Collins noticed a slender slugger named Ted Williams. Collins, a veteran of 25 major league seasons, contacted the Red Sox and signed both players.

**WILLIAMS THE PITCHER:** Teddy Ballgame appeared in one game and pitched two innings during his 19-year career. He hurled the final two frames in a 12-1 loss to the Detroit Tigers. He allowed one run on three hits, but did strike out slugger Rudy York.

**WILLIAMS THE MGR.:** Williams managed the Washington Senators from 1969 to 1971, compiling a record of 219-264. His best season with the Senators came in 1969, when his club finished 86-76 and fourth in the American League East. He was named manager of the year. He remained with the franchise when it moved to Texas in 1972 and became known as the Rangers. His record there: 54-100.

**MARRIAGES:** Williams was married three times. His first marriage to Doris Soule produced a daughter, Barbara Joyce. That marriage ended in 1955. In 1961, he married Lee

Howard, a model from Chicago. They divorced in 1967. In 1968, Williams married Delores Wettach. The pair had two children, John-Henry (1968) and Claudia (1971). This marriage ended in 1972. In all three divorces, official papers used the word "cruelty" on Williams' part. Williams then lived with Louise Kaufman for 20 years until her death in 1993.

**MILITARY SERVICE:** Williams served as a U.S. Marine Corps pilot during World War II and the Korean War. During WW II, he was a flight instructor in Pensacola, FL. He returned to duty in 1953 during the Korean War. Overall, he flew 38 combat missions before being pulled from flight status in June of 1953 after an old ear infection acted up.

**FAVORITE QUOTE:** "A man has to have goals—for a day, for a lifetime—and that was mine, to have people say, 'There goes Ted Williams, the greatest hitter who ever lived.'"

**FAST FACT:** The pitcher Williams had the most success with, home-run wise, was Virgil Trucks of the Tigers, Browns and White Sox with 12. He roughed up Bob Feller of the Indians and Ned Garver of the Browns, Tigers and Athletics for 10 apiece. Jim Bunning of the Tigers, Fred Hutchinson of the Tigers and Early Wynn of the Senators, Indians and White Sox each yielded 8.

**DID YOU KNOW?** Williams actually retired after the 1954 season, when he batted .345, hit 29 homers and led the league in on-base percentage (.497) and slugging percentage (.608) in 117 games. Hefty monthly alimony and child support payments from his first divorce forced Williams to change his mind, so he signed with the Red Sox for $60,000 on May 13, 1955 to play the rest of the season. Also, Williams never collected 200 or more hits in a season.

**HALL OF FAME:** Class of 1966.

One of Ted's proudest moments came in the 1941 All-Star Game when he hit a two-out, bottom-of-the-ninth, three-run homer to lift the American League to a dramatic 6-5 win. Waiting for Ted at home is Joe DiMaggio (No. 5).

## CHAPTER 3

# Joe's Streak Comes to an End

Two spectacular plays by an underrated third baseman, a bad hop at short, two pitchers who combined for just 21 victories in 1941 and even a taxi cab driver were responsible for the end of Joe DiMaggio's 56-game hitting streak in Cleveland on July 17.

Cleveland third baseman Kenny Keltner's (above) two tremendous plays robbed Joe of two hits, thus ending the record 56-game hitting streak.

The third baseman was Kenny Keltner. The bad-hop grounder was handled perfectly by shortstop Lou Boudreau. The two pitchers were veteran lefty Al Smith and young righty Jim Bagby, who posted records of 12-13 and 9-15, respectively, in 1941.

The name of the taxi cab driver remains unknown, but he picked up DiMaggio and his Yankee roommate, pitcher Lefty Gomez, for the ride to Cleveland's Municipal Stadium. The cabbie, who recognized "The Yankee Clipper," turned to DiMaggio and said he had a "hunch" the hitting streak would be halted that evening at 56. DiMaggio ignored the cabbie, but Gomez, the Yankees' starting pitcher that night, verbally blasted him, saying, "You're full of bunk." Sitting at a stop light, Gomez quickly ushered DiMaggio out of the cab and the two walked the rest of the way to the stadium.

DiMaggio and the cabbie met again more than 30 years later. "He apologized and he was serious," Joe said. "I felt awful. He apparently spent his whole life thinking he really jinxed me. I told him he hadn't. My number was just up that night."

DiMaggio's 56-game streak actually broke two records by Willie Keeler of the then-National League Baltimore Orioles. Keeler hit in 45 straight, but that mark was achieved over two seasons (1896-87). Keeler, an outfielder who posted a .341 career batting average over 19 seasons (1892-1910), also set the single-season record of 44 in 1897. The Hall of Fame outfielder collected a base hit in the final game of the 1896 season, then hit safely in 44 straight at the start of the 1897 campaign. Through the 2009 season, he still shared the National League single-season mark of 44 with Pete Rose of the Cincinnati Reds, who tied the record in 1978.

Keeler passed away in 1923 at the age of 51, so he didn't have the opportunity to see his record shattered by DiMaggio.

A crowd of nearly 70,000 jammed Municipal Stadium that July 17 night to see if Joe could extend his streak to 57.

In the first inning against Indian starter Smith, DiMaggio ripped a 1-0 pitch past third base, but Keltner, playing deep and guarding the line, backhanded the ball and made a perfect throw to first for the out.

DiMaggio walked in the fourth. In the seventh against Bagby, Joe again hit a shot to third, but again Keltner was there and threw the bewildered DiMaggio out by a half step.

"When Joe came up in the eighth, the bases were loaded and the count stood at 1-1," recalled Hall of Fame pitcher Bob Feller, who watched the drama unfold from the Cleveland dugout that night.

"A lot of people forget what happened," Feller continued. "Joe hit a wicked grounder to Boudreau at short, but at the very last second, the ball took a bad bounce, but Lou barehanded the ball and tossed it to our second baseman, Ray Mack, to start a double-play."

"Joe showed absolutely no emotions going back to the dugout," Feller recalled. "He ran out every ball very hard that night. He knew the streak was over."

But hold on! Going into the bottom of the ninth, the Yankees held a 4-1 lead, but Gomez got into trouble and the Indians closed the count to 4-3, thanks to a two-run triple by pinch-hitter Larry Rosenthal, a .209 hitter.

"Had Rosenthal been a little faster, he may have scored to tie the game," Feller recalled.

With the tying run standing 90-feet from home and no outs, Yankee skipper Joe McCarthy went to the bull pen and brought in righty Johnny Murphy, who saved a league-leading 15 games and posted a 1.98 earned-run-average that season.

Up to the plate came .294 hitter Hal Trosky, a lefty. If Trosky could have knocked the ball through the drawn-in Yankee infield, the Indians could have tied the game, possibly giving DiMaggio another at-bat in the 10th. Trosky, however, grounded out to first.

With Rosenthal still at third, lefty Clarence Campbell, a .250 hitter, pinch-hit for Bagby. Campbell hit a hard grounder to the mound, where Murphy knocked the ball down, then caught Rosenthal in a run-down between third and home for the second out. Campbell, meanwhile, stayed at first and made no attempt to advance to second base during the run-down play.

With two outs, the Indians' lead-off hitter, lefty Roy Weatherly (.289), was DiMaggio's last hope for another at-bat in the 10th. Yankee first baseman Johnny Sturm was holding base-runner Campbell at first. Weatherly hit a sharp grounder right at Sturm, who fielded the ball cleanly and stepped on first to end the game. Had Sturm been playing off the first-base bag, Weatherly's hit would have rolled down the right-field line and Campbell would have probably scored to tie the game at 4.

The Streak was over at 56, but DiMaggio started another hitting streak of 16 games the next night. Had he hit safely in Game 57, Joe would have extended his streak to 73. That 16-game streak was halted on Aug. 3 at Yankee Stadium in a 2-0 loss to the St. Louis Browns.

"During Joe's streak, there were a few questionable calls," Feller said. "He was given the benefit of the doubt by the official scorers on plays that could have been ruled errors. But Joe's streak was good for baseball. People talked about it all the time and it put people in the stands."

Two hit balls by DiMaggio stood out as "questionable calls." On June 17 (Game 30) at home against the White Sox, Joe hit a grounder to shortstop Luke Appling. The ball took a weird bounce and hit Appling in the shoulder. Official scorekeeper Dan Daniel, a friend of DiMaggio's, ruled it a hit.

On the very next day (Game 31), Appling bobbled a grounder by a hitless DiMaggio in the seventh. Daniel again scored it a hit, which raised quite a few eyebrows.

The star of the game on July 17 in Cleveland, though, was Keltner, who received a police escort following the contest due to the many DiMaggio fans in the stands that night.

"My own fans booed me," Keltner recalled. "They wanted Joe's streak to continue."

The 6-foot, 190-pound Keltner was a seven-time All-Star during his 13 seasons, 12 with the Indians (1937-44, 1946-49) and one with Boston (1950). A native of Milwaukee, the right-handed swinger had a career batting average of .276 with 163 homers and 852 RBIs. He averaged only 13 errors per season and participated in 306 double-plays, while posting a .965 fielding percentage.

"Kenny was by far one of the top third basemen during the 1940s," former Red Sox shortstop Johnny Pesky said. "He was a vacuum cleaner. He had great range, and a strong and accurate arm. I wasn't in the majors in 1941, but when I joined the Red Sox in 1942, I got a first-hand look at Kenny and he was definitely one of the best. And he was such a wonderful person."

Years later, DiMaggio asked Keltner why he played so deep and hugged the third-base line that night, almost to the point where the third baseman was playing a short left field. Keltner's reply: "I knew you weren't going to bunt and I covered the line to stop an extra-base hit."

Keltner passed away in 1991 at the age of 75 in New Berlin, WI.

For DiMaggio, the streak was a true-life drama every day.

"The pressure of getting a hit in 56 straight games must have been unbearable," former Red Sox second baseman and Hall of Famer Bobby Doerr said. "Just think of it."

DiMaggio's personal diary states that. "If I thought this would be taking place, I would have stopped the hitting streak at 40," DiMaggio wrote, referring to the pressure and attention The Streak was given on a daily basis by the media.

Gomez, said, "Nothing seemed to be bothering him (during The Streak), but he must have been dying inside."

"When his streak ended that night in Cleveland," Feller said, "it didn't appear to be that big of a deal to him. Maybe he was relieved it was over. He showed no emotion."

Others, including his late brother, Dom of the Red Sox, said, "Joe was upset when The Streak ended."

The Streak started on May 15 with a harmless single at Yankee Stadium during a 13-1 loss to the White Sox. Ironically, on the same day, his rival and good friend Ted Williams started a 23-game hitting streak at Fenway Park in a 6-4 loss to the Indians. That 23-game streak, which ended June 8 in a 5-3 win against the White Sox, helped propel Williams to his .406 batting average that season.

When the two streaks started, Williams was hitting .339, Joe .304. During the parallel 23-game streaks, Williams went 43-for-88 for a .489 average, DiMaggio 32-for-87, a .368 clip.

DiMaggio had a few close calls. On May 24, for example, a hitless DiMaggio approached the batter's box in the seventh inning with two outs and runners on second and third. With the Red Sox clinging to a 6-5 lead, Boston Manager Joe Cronin decided to pitch to DiMaggio instead of intentionally walking him. Sure enough, DiMaggio came through, lining a game-winning single to left off southpaw Earl Johnson. Had Cronin walked DiMaggio, the streak would have ended at nine games.

In another game, DiMaggio was scheduled to hit fourth in the eighth inning during a lopsided Yankee win. With one out and a runner on first, Tommy Henrich stepped to the plate. To avoid possibly grounding into a double-play, Henrich received permission from Manager McCarthy to drop down a bunt so DiMaggio would get one last turn at the plate. Sure enough, DiMaggio came through with a single.

When The Streak did end in Cleveland, DiMaggio asked teammate and shortstop Phil Rizzuto to wait for him so the two could walk back to the hotel together. Once the two reached the hotel, Joe, who had left his wallet in his room, asked Phil for some cash. Rizzuto recalled that he had $18. DiMaggio took the money, sent Rizzuto to his room and sat in a bar drinking with strangers.

**DURING THE STREAK, A SONG, "JOLTIN' JOE DIMAGGIO," WAS PERFORMED BY THE LES BROWN BAND:**

WHO STARTED BASEBALL'S FAMOUS STREAK
THAT'S GOT US ALL AGLOW,
HE'S JUST A MAN AND NOT A FREAK
JOLTING JOE DIMAGGIO.
JOE... JOE...DIMAGGIO
WE WANT YOU ON OUR SIDE.

FROM COAST TO COAST, THAT'S ALL YOU HEAR
OF JOE THE ONE-MAN SHOW,
HE'S GLORIFIED THE HORSEHIDE SPHERE
JOLTING JOE DIMAGGIO.
JOE... JOE...DIMAGGIO
WE WANT YOU ON OUR SIDE.

HE'LL LIVE IN BASEBALL'S HALL OF FAME
HE GOT THERE BLOW-BY-BLOW,
OUR KIDS WILL TELL THEIR KIDS HIS NAME,
JOLTING JOE DIMAGGIO.

# THE STREAK GAME-BY-GAME

A game-by-game recap of Joe DiMaggio's record 56-game hitting streak in **1941**:

| GAME/DATE | DIMAGGIO AT THE PLATE |
| --- | --- |
| 1 (5-15) | In a 13-1 loss to the White Sox, Joe goes 1-for-4 with an RBI against pitcher Eddie Smith. |
| 2 (5-16) | Joe goes 2-4 with a triple, homer and RBI in a 6-5 win over Thornton Lee and the White Sox. |
| 3 (5-17) | White Sox pitcher Johnny Rigney beats the Yankees, 3-2, but Joe goes 1-3. |
| 4 (5-18) | Against the Browns, Joe goes 2-2 against Bob Harris and 1-1 against Johnny Niggeling in a 12-2 Yankee win. |
| 5 (5-19) | Joe manages a double in three at-bats in a 5-1 loss to Denny Galehouse and the Browns. |
| 6 (5-20) | In the series finale, Joe goes 1-5 with an RBI in a 10-9 win over the Browns and Elden Auker. |

7 (5-21)   Against the Tigers, Joe goes a combined 2-5 with an RBI vs. Schoolboy Rowe and Al Benton in a 5-4 Yankee win.

8 (5-22)   Joe goes 1-4 with an RBI against the Tigers' Archie McKain in a 6-5 New York win.

9 (5-23)   In a wild 9-9 tie against the Red Sox, Joe goes 1-5 with 2 RBIs against Dick Newsome.

10 (5-24)  Joe knocks in 2 runs and goes 1-4 against Earl Johnson in a 7-6 Yankee win over the Bosox.

11 (5-25)  The Red Sox's Lefty Grove beats the Yanks, 10-3, but Joe manages a single in 4 at-bats.

12 (5-27)  Big day at the plate for Joe, with a 3-5 performance, 3 runs, a homer and 3 RBIs against Ken Chase, Red Anderson and Alex Carrasquel in a 10-8 win over the Senators.

13 (5-28)  Joe triples and scores a run in 4 at-bats against the Senators' Sid Hudson in a 6-5 Yankee win.

14 (5-29)  In a 2-2 tie vs. the Senators and pitcher Steve Sundra, Joe goes 1-3.

15 (5-30)  Joe manages a single in 2 at-bats in a 4-3 win over the Red Sox and Earl Johnson.

| | |
|---|---|
| 16 (5-30) | In the second game of the double-header, Joe goes 1-3 with a double in a humiliating 13-0 loss to the Red Sox and Mickey Harris. |
| 17 (6-1) | Joe goes 1-4 in a tight 2-0 win over the Indians and Al Milnar. |
| 18 (6-1) | In the second half of the twin-bill, Joe posts another 1-4 effort in a 5-3 victory over the Indians' Mel Harder. |
| 19 (6-2) | Joe collects a single and double in 4 at-bats against Bob Feller, who posted a 7-5 win. |
| 20 (6-3) | A homer and 1 RBI in 4 at-bats is all Joe can do against Dizzy Trout in a 4-2 Tiger victory. |
| 21 (6-5) | After an off day due to rain, Hal Newhouser and the Tigers complete a two-game sweep of the Yankees with a 5-4 triumph. Joe goes 1-5 with an RBI. |
| 22 (6-7) | Joe collects a single each off Bob Muncrief, Johnny Allen and George Caster in a 3-5 performance as the Yanks beat the Browns, 11-7. |
| 23 (6-8) | Joe's 2 homers, 4 RBIs and 3 runs scored power the Yankees to a 9-3 win over Elden Auker and the Browns. |

| | |
|---|---|
| 24 (6-8) | In the nightcap of the double-header, Joe homers again, adds a double and drives in 3 runs against George Caster and Jack Kramer in the Yankees' 8–3 victory. |
| 25 (6-10) | Joe manages a 1-5 performance against Johnny Rigney in the New Yorkers' 8–3 win over the White Sox. |
| 26 (6-12) | The Yankees beat the White Sox again, this time 3–2, thanks to Joe's 2-4 effort, homer and RBI. |
| 27 (6-14) | The Yankees open a three-game series vs. the Indians with a 4–1 win over Bob Feller. Joe goes 1-2 with a double and RBI. |
| 28 (6-15) | Joe homers in 3 at-bats, has an RBI and run scored in a 3–2 victory over Jim Bagby and the Tribe. |
| 29 (6-16) | The Yankees make it three straight over the Indians and eight overall with a 6–4 win over Al Milnar. Joe doubles in 5 at-bats. |
| 30 (6-17) | Johnny Rigney and the White Sox stopped the Yanks' eight-game win streak with an 8–7 win. Joe goes 1-4. |

| | |
|---|---|
| 31 (6-18) | Joe manages a single in 3 at-bats in a 3-2 loss to Thornton Lee and the White Sox. |
| 32 (6-19) | Joe goes 3-3 with a homer and 2 RBIs against the White Sox's Eddie Smith and Buck Ross in a 7-2 Yankee win. |
| 33 (6-20) | A 4-hit day by Joe, 3 runs scored, a double and RBI power the Yankees to an easy 14-4 win over the Tigers' Bobo Newsom and Archie McKain. |
| 34 (6-21) | The Tigers avenge the 14-4 loss the previous day as Dizzy Trout beats the Yanks, 7-2. Joe manages a 1-4 effort with an RBI. |
| 35 (6-22) | A double, homer and 2 RBIs by Joe lifts the Yanks to a 5-4 win over the Tigers' Hal Newhouser and Bobo Newsom. |
| 36 (6-24) | The Yanks open a three-game series against the Browns with a 9-1 win over Bob Muncrief. Joe goes 1-4. |
| 37 (6-25) | Joe goes 1-4, a 3-run homer, in a 7-5 Yankee win over the Browns' Denny Galehouse. |
| 38 (6-26) | A double and RBI by Joe helps the Yanks beat the Browns and Elden Auker, 4-1, to complete a three-game series sweep. |

| | |
|---|---|
| 39 (6-27) | Joe collects 2 hits, including a 2-run homer, but the Yanks fall, 7-6, to Chubby Dean and the Athletics. |
| 40 (6-28) | Joe is the talk of baseball as he closes in on the major league record held by Baltimore's Willie Keeler, who hit safely in 45 straight games during portions of the 1896 and 1897 seasons. He moves within one game of tying the modern-day record of 41 set by George Sisler of the Browns in 1922. Joe responds with a 2-5 effort against Johnny Babich and Lum Harris in a 7-4 win over the Athletics. |
| 41 (6-29) | Joe ties George Sisler's record of 41 straight games with a hit in the first game of a doubleheader, going 1-4 with a double against Dutch Leonard in a 9-4 win over the Senators. |
| 42 (6-29) | Joe breaks Sisler's record in the second game of the double-header by going 1-5 against Red Anderson in a 7-5 Yankee win. |
| 43 (7-1) | In another double-header, Joe goes 2-4 with an RBI against the Red Sox's Mickey Harris and Mike Ryba in a 7-2 triumph. |
| 44 (7-1) | In the nightcap against Jack Wilson and the Red Sox, Joe goes 1-3 with an RBI in a 9-2 |

victory. The hit enabled DiMaggio to tie Willie Keeler's single-season record of 44 set in 1897. Keeler, who played for Baltimore, actually hit in 45 straight because he got a single in the Orioles' final game of the 1896 season.

Joe tied Willie Keeler's single-season record of hitting safely in 44 consecutive games on July 1, 1941 against Boston.

| | |
|---|---|
| 45 (7-2) | Joe ties Willie Keeler's record of 45 in grand style with a three-run homer off the Red Sox's Dick Newsome. Yanks win, 8-4. |
| 46 (7-5) | After a two-day break, Joe surpasses Keeler's streak of 45 and sets a new record for hitting safely in his 46th straight game with a 2-run homer off the Athletics' Phil Marchildon in a 10-5 runaway. |
| 47 (7-6) | In the first game of a twin-bill against the Athletics, Joe goes 4-5 with a double and 2 RBIs in an 8-4 win against Johnny Babich and Bump Hadley. |
| 48 (7-6) | Joe's record streak continues to grow in the second game as he goes 2-4 with a triple and 2 RBIs off Jack Knott in a 3-1 win. |
| 49 (7-10) | Following the All-Star break, Joe goes back to work on his streak with a 1-2 effort off Johnny Niggeling in a 1-0 win over the Browns. The victory was the Yankees' 10th straight. |
| 50 (7-11) | The Browns' Bob Harris and Jack Kramer can't slow down the Yankee Clipper as he goes 4-5 with a homer and 2 RBIs in a 6-2 New York win. |

51 (7-12)   Joe goes 2-5 with a double and RBI against the Browns' Elden Auker and Bob Muncrief as the Yankees win their 12th straight, 7-5.

52 (7-13)   "How long can this streak last?" people asked. Could Joe match and surpass his 61-game hitting streak, which he achieved with the San Francisco Seals of the Pacific Coast League in 1933? The streak reaches 52 with a 3-4 performance in an 8-1 win over the White Sox and pitchers Ted Lyons and Jack Hallett.

53 (7-14)   Joes goes 1-4 in a 1-0 win over the White Sox and Thornton Lee. The victory was the Yankees' 14th straight and 18th in the past 19 games.

54 (7-14)   A 1-3 effort against the White Sox's Johnny Rigney keeps the streak alive, but the Yankees fall, 7-1.

55 (7-15)   Joe collects 2 hits and drives in a pair of runs as the Yanks beat the White Sox and Eddie Smith.

56 (7-16)   A 3-4 performance with 3 runs scored runs the streak to 56. This time it comes in Cleveland in a 10-3 win over Al Milnar and Joe Krakauskas.

Joe's 91st and final hit during the 56-game streak, a single against Cleveland's Joe Krakauskas on July 16, 1941.

57 (7-17)   The Streak ended in Cleveland, thanks to a pair of outstanding defensive plays by third baseman Kenny Keltner, a third one by shortstop Lou Boudreau and the pitching of Al Smith and Jim Bagby. The Yankees won the game, however, 4-3. On July 18, the day after The Streak ended, Joe went on to hit safely in 16 straight games.

## HITTING STREAK TIDBITS

- During The Streak, DiMaggio went 91-for-223, an average of .408.

- He scored 56 runs, had 55 runs-batted-in, 15 homers, 16 doubles, 4 triples.

- His slugging percentage was an incredible .717.

- The Yankees posted a 41-13-2 record.

- When the hitting streak started, the Yankees had a record of 14-15. When it ended, they were 56-27-2. They eventually finished 101-53-2 and beat the Brooklyn Dodgers in five World Series games.

- Joe had 22 multi-hit games, including four 4-hit games and six 3-hit games.

- Against Hall of Fame pitchers, Joe was 2-for-3 against Chicago's Ted Lyons, 3-for-6 against Cleveland's Bob Feller, 1-for-4 against Boston's Lefty Grove and 2-for-9 against Detroit's Hal Newhouser.

# JOE VS. THE OPPONENTS DURING 'THE STREAK'

| Opponent | AB | R | H | 2B | 3B | HR | RBI | AVG. |
|---|---|---|---|---|---|---|---|---|
| Boston Red Sox | 30 | 5 | 9 | 1 | 0 | 1 | 9 | .300 |
| Chicago White Sox | 45 | 11 | 19 | 1 | 1 | 3 | 7 | .423 |
| Cleveland Indians | 26 | 7 | 10 | 4 | 0 | 1 | 2 | .385 |
| Detroit Tigers | 32 | 6 | 12 | 2 | 1 | 2 | 8 | .440 |
| Philadelphia Athletics | 21 | 6 | 11 | 2 | 1 | 2 | 8 | .524 |
| St. Louis Browns | 48 | 14 | 22 | 5 | 0 | 5 | 17 | 458 |
| Washington Senators | 21 | 7 | 8 | 1 | 1 | 1 | 4 | .381 |
| **Totals** | **223** | **56** | **91** | **16** | **4** | **15** | **55** | **.408** |

# MAJOR LEAGUE HITTING STREAKS

Thirteen major league players have had consecutive hitting streaks of 35 or more games 15 times. George Sisler (1922 and 1924-25) and Ty Cobb (1911 and 1917) both reached the mark twice. Here's a list of players who have hit safely in 35 or more games through the 2009 season:

| PLAYER | TEAM (YEAR) | STREAK |
| --- | --- | --- |
| Joe DiMaggio | New York Yankees (1941) | 56 |
| Willie Keeler | Baltimore Orioles (1896-97) | 45 |
| Pete Rose | Cincinnati Reds (1978) | 44 |
| Bill Dahlen | Chicago Colts (1894) | 42 |
| George Sisler | St. Louis Browns (1922) | 41 |
| Ty Cobb | Detroit Tigers (1911) | 40 |
| Paul Molitor | Milwaukee Brewers (1987) | 39 |
| Jimmy Rollins | Philadelphia Phillies (2005-06) | 38 |
| Tommy Holmes | Boston Braves (1945) | 37 |
| Gene DeMontreville | Washington Senators (1896-97) | 36 |
| Fred Clarke | Louisville Cardinals (1895) | 35 |
| Ty Cobb | Detroit Tigers (1917) | 35 |

| | | |
|---|---|---|
| George Sisler | St. Louis Browns (1924-25) | 35 |
| Luis Castillo | Florida Marlins (2002) | 35 |
| Chase Utley | Philadelphia Phillies (2006) | 35 |

## MINOR LEAGUE HITTING STREAKS

DiMaggio ranks second in the minor-league record books with a 61-game streak.

| PLAYER | LEAGUE (YEAR) | STREAK |
|---|---|---|
| Joe Wilhoit | Western League (1919) | 69 |
| Joe DiMaggio | Pacific Coast League (1933) | 61 |
| Roman Mejias | Big State League (1954) | 55 |
| Otto Pahlman | Ilinois-Iowa-Indiana (1922) | 50 |

**Note:** Joe Wilhoit actually set the minor-league hit streak record *after* he completed his major league career. He played four seasons with the Braves, Pirates, Giants and Red Sox, compiling a career average of .257 with three homers and 73 RBIs. Between June 14 and Aug. 19, 1919, he hit safely in 69 games for the Wichita Witches of the Western League. During his streak, he batted .512, going 153-for-299. He passed away in 1930 at the age of 45.

## CHAPTER 4

# Ted Shoots for .400 on Final Day

To burn off energy, a nervous Ted Williams walked the streets of Philadelphia. The date was Sept. 27, 1941. Earlier that day, Williams had a double in four at-bats against the Athletics in a 4-1 Red Sox victory. More important, though, was the fact his batting average dipped below the magical .400 mark for the first time since July 24 at Fenway Park where a 2-for-5 effort dropped him to .397.

Entering the final day of the season—a Sept. 28 double-header in Philly—Williams' average stood at .39955.

"I was very nervous," Williams recalled years later. "I walked and walked, just to get the jitters out of my system."

Williams stopped at several drug stores during his walking tour of Philly to have his favorite treat, a malt. He usually went to bed at 10 p.m., but returned to the hotel lobby at 10:30. He was greeted by his manager, Joe Cronin.

Would Major League Baseball round up Williams' .39955 to .400? Cronin said yes, so when Williams walked in, he suggested that his left fielder "sit out" the double-header the next day.

Ted is the youngest—and last —player to hit above the magical .400 mark, achieving his .406 average in 1941 at the age of 23.

Williams said no, saying if he was going to clear the .400 mark, he "wanted to do it all the way. I never wanted anything harder in my life, but I wanted to do it the right way."

As a result, Cronin wrote Williams' name on his lineup card for Game 1.

"It didn't seem to me or some of the other players that it was a big deal," recalled Red Sox second baseman Bobby Doerr. "There really wasn't a lot of talk about .400" because in 1930 Bill Terry of the New York Giants posted a .401 average. "Hitting .400 wasn't that big of a novelty. Of course, now it is."

Terry spent 14 seasons (1923-36) with the New York Giants, compiling a career batting average of .341. The Hall of Fame first baseman collected a National League-record 254 hits en route to his .401 season in 1930. The record for most hits in a season through 2009 was held by Seattle's Ichiro Suzuki, who hammered out 262 in 2004.

A change in the sacrifice fly rule worked against Williams during his pursuit of .400 in 1941. From 1926-30, a batter was NOT charged with an at-bat if he advanced any runner from one base to another. Terry's .401 benefited from this rule as he collected 19 sacrifice hits.

From 1940 to 1953, a batter WAS charged with an at-bat even if he drove home a run with a (sacrifice) fly. In 1941, Williams had six sacrifice flies, although his official statistics list him with none because of the rule. By subtracting the six sacrifice flies, Williams would have had 450 official at-bats instead of 456. As a result, the slugger's final average would have been .411 and the last-day heroics in Philadelphia would not have been necessary. In 1954, baseball reinstated the sacrifice fly as it is known today—no official at-bat.

"That definitely worked against Ted," Doerr said. "But it was the rule."

"I think a lot of guys would have sat out like Cronin suggested, but not Ted," Doerr said. "He wasn't going to take the easy way out. He was nervous, but he was motivated and charged up."

"If you knew Ted, you knew he was a very determined person. He was a very proud person. Everything he did was to perfection."

"We all figured Ted would get his hits and climb above .400. People were aware of what was at stake, but to us it wasn't a big deal," Doerr said.

One person who didn't think Williams could hold up to the pressure that final day was Philadelphia coach Al Simmons, who batted a career-high .390 in 1930 for the Athletics. Prior to the double-header, Simmons strolled over to Williams and told him he couldn't stay at .400 with a boat paddle. Williams laughed it off.

Williams, who batted .327 his rookie season in 1939 and .344 in 1940, was up to the challenge. In the opener that afternoon, a 12-11 Red Sox win, he collected three singles and his 37th league-leading homer in five at-bats to raise his average to .404.

"My hands were shaking," Williams said of his first at-bat in the Sunday afternoon opener.

On the mound was 20-year-old Dick Fowler (1-2, 3.38 ERA in four games), a right-handed rookie who was called up late in the season. Williams greeted Fowler with a line-drive to right for a base hit, then followed that in the third with a home run. Fowler, who posted a 66-79 record in 10 seasons with the Athletics, was done for the day.

In the sixth, Williams faced Porter Vaughn (0-2, 7.94 ERA). Williams made easy work of the lefty, lacing a single to center.

In the seventh, Williams came to the plate with a runner on first. Philadelphia Manager Connie Mack, willing to do anything to stop Williams, pulled his first baseman, Bob Johnson, off the bag and positioned him on the outfield grass. On a 3-2 pitch, Vaughn fed Williams a curve on the outside corner of the plate. Williams took a mighty swing and ripped a single to right, exactly in the spot Johnson had vacated. Williams was a perfect 4-for-4, raising his average to .405. When he made his fifth appearance at the plate, Williams reached on an error.

Cronin, concerned about the bad shadows at home plate at Shibe Park, suggested that Williams, now at .404, sit out the second game, but again, his slugger would have none of it. "The record's no good unless it's made in all the games," Williams said.

In the nightcap, a 7-1 Red Sox loss, Williams singled and doubled in three plate appearances against another rookie, Fred Caligiuri (2-2, 2.93 ERA in five games). Two innings later, he popped out minutes before the game was called because of darkness to complete the season at .406. Although Williams went 2-for-3 against Caligiuri, a 21-year-old righty, the pitcher did pick up the victory, going the distance while allowing six hits.

For Williams, who hit .428 at Fenway and .380 on the road that season, he became the youngest player (age 23) to reach the .400 mark. Ty Cobb of Detroit and Joe Jackson of the White Sox were both 24 when they hit .420 and .411, respectively, in 1911.

Years later, Williams said, "Everything I hit fell in. Every break I could get I got."

"What a thrill it was to watch Ted go 6-for-8 that day," Doerr said. "It was remarkable."

"At the time, I don't think people really realized what an amazing accomplishment it was," said Red Sox center fielder Dom DiMaggio prior to his death in May of 2009. "It's been a lifetime since there's been a .400 hitter. And the chances of another .400 is slim, unless they change some rules."

"The fielding is better today, too," Dom said. "I'm not going to say that about the pitching, though. There are a wealth of pitchers from my day who would have easily held their own against today's hitters."

Former Hall of Fame historian, the late Jerome Holtzman, who covered MLB for nearly 60 years for the *Chicago Tribune* and *Chicago Sun Times*, wrote, Williams' last-day heroics were "a demonstration of courage and his supreme confidence in his ability."

"Williams could have benched himself and protected his average," Holtzman wrote. "Joe Cronin and several teammates encouraged him to sit out, but Williams was in quest of immortality."

"You could see Ted's determination," recalled the late Les McCrabb before his death in October of 2008. "I don't think any pitcher or pitchers could have prevented Ted from getting that .400."

McCrabb, a pitcher for Philadelphia, was in the Athletics' dugout that final day of the 1941 season watching history unfold. "Connie Mack (the Athletics' managers) and our pitchers really wanted to spoil Ted's day. But we're talking about Ted Williams, the greatest hitter ever."

"I contributed to Ted's .400," McCrabb added with a laugh. "He hit three home runs off me that season."

Williams did miss winning the Triple Crown as the Yankees' Joe DiMaggio finished with 125 runs-batted-in compared to Williams' 120. Several weeks later, DiMaggio was named the American League's Most Valuable Player. DiMaggio garnered 15 first-place votes to Williams' 8. Point-wise, DiMaggio collected 291 points to Williams' 254. DiMaggio, who had hit in 56 consecutive games that season, hit .357 and led the Yankees to 101 regular-season wins and a five-game World Series victory over the Brooklyn Dodgers. The Red Sox finished second with an 84-70 record.

Williams actually hit .400 two more times after he returned from the Korean War, but he fell far short of the necessary at-bats to be considered a contender for a batting title. In 1952, he went 4-for-10 for an even .400. The following season, he posted a .407 mark, going 37-for-91.

# A SUMMARY OF TED'S .406 SEASON

A brief, month-by-month summary of Ted Williams' .406 season:

### APRIL

| | |
|---|---|
| 15TH | Ted, appearing as a pinch-hitter, singles in his only at-bat against the Senators.<br>**Average:** 1.000 |
| 22ND | Williams goes 2-for-4 with a single and double vs. the Senators.<br>**Average:** .444 |
| 29TH | A homer and double in three at-bats against the Tigers boosts his average above .450.<br>**Average:** .462 |
| 30TH | Ted's average tumbles below .400 with a 1-5 effort at Detroit.<br>**Average:** .389 |

**Ted's totals to date: 7-for-18, .389**

### MAY

| | |
|---|---|
| 1ST-3RD | Ted suffers through a three-game slump at Detroit and Cleveland, going just 2-for-11.<br>**Average:** .310 |

| | |
|---|---|
| 11TH | Williams goes on a terror over the next three games, despite several rainouts, going 3-for-6 at New York.<br>**Average: .386** |
| 13TH-16TH | Another slump (3-for-16) at Chicago and Cleveland drops Ted's average to its lowest mark for the remainder of the season.<br>**Average: .333** |
| 24TH-25TH | Williams goes 6-for-8 with five singles and a double at home against the Yankees. His average will remain above .400 until July 6 (.399).<br>**Average: .404** |
| 27TH-30TH | Ted swings his bat at a torrid pace, going 11-for-20 over the next six games at Philly and New York.<br>**Average: .429** |

Ted's totals to date: 51-for-119, .429

**JUNE**

| | |
|---|---|
| 1ST-6TH | Williams continues to swing a hot bat with four multiple-hit games at home against the Tigers, Indians and White Sox.<br>**Average: .436** |

| | |
|---|---|
| 7TH-12TH | Ted's bat cools off, going 3-for-16 at home vs. the White Sox and Browns.<br>**Average:** .410 |
| 14TH-15TH | A 7-for-11 three-game series at Chicago puts Williams back on track.<br>**Average:** .425 |
| 17TH-29TH | Williams' average takes a steady dive from .425 with a 14-for-42 performance (.333) at the plate.<br>**Average:** .404 |

**Ted's totals to date: 86-for-213, .404**

## JULY

| | |
|---|---|
| 1ST-2ND | A 3-for-9 effort in three games at home against the New Yorkers drops Ted's average to its lowest mark since May 24 when he was batting .383.<br>**Average:** .401 |
| 6TH | Williams' 1-for-4 performance at Washington has people questioning his ability to maintain a .400 pace.<br>**Average:** .399 |
| 11TH-24TH | Tough times for Teddy Ballgame—by his standard—over the next two weeks, as his average remains in the .390s.<br>**Average:** .397 |

| | |
|---|---|
| 25TH-27TH | A 7-for-10 three-game series at Cleveland has Ted back in the .400s.<br>**Average:** .408 |

Ted's totals to date: 113-for-276, .409.

## AUGUST

| | |
|---|---|
| 2ND | Williams starts the new month off with a single and double in three at-bats at Detroit.<br>**Average:** .412 |
| 3RD-15TH | Williams bats .367 the first half of the month, going 18-for-49. His seasonal average ranges from .403 to .413.<br>**Average:** .405 |
| 16TH-31ST | Ted enjoys seven multiple-hit games, but also goes hitless in five others. Highlights include a 3-for-5 at home against the Senators and a four-hit game vs. the Browns. Can the Splendid Splinter hold on with one month left to play?<br>**Average:** .407 |

Ted's totals to date: 156-383, .407.

## SEPTEMBER

| | |
|---|---|
| 1ST-27TH | Ted manages to keep his average in the .405 to .413 range until Sept. 27, when his average dips to .39955 following a 2-for-10 effort in a three-game series against Washington and a 1-for-4 day vs. Philadelphia.<br>**Average:** .39955 |
| 28TH | On the final day of the season, Williams, realizing his .39955 would round up to .400 if he didn't take the field, insists on playing. He didn't disappoint his fans, going 4-for-5 in the first game to raise his average to .404, then 2-for-3 in the second game against Philadelphia to finish at **.406**. |

## TED'S FINAL 1941 TOTALS

Games: 143

Hits/at bats: 185-for-456;
Average: .406

Runs: 135
Runs-batted-in: 120

Doubles: 33
Triples: 3
Home runs: 37

Base-on-balls: 147

Strikeouts: 27

On-base percentage: .553

Slugging percentage: .735

Zero-hit games: 38

One-hit games 56

Two-hit games: 34

Three-hit games: 15

Four-hit games: 4

Longest hit streak: 23 games

Longest hitless streak: 2 games (several times)

## TED HOME & AWAY IN 1941

Home: .428 (104-for-243, 19 hrs.)

Road: .380 (81-for-213, 18 hrs.)

# TED VS. AL OPPONENTS DURING 1941

| OPPONENT | AB | R | H | HR | RBI | AVG. |
|---|---|---|---|---|---|---|
| Chicago White Sox | 69 | 17 | 26 | 7 | 17 | .377 |
| Cleveland Indians | 58 | 22 | 24 | 3 | 9 | .414 |
| Detroit Tigers | 74 | 21 | 25 | 5 | 19 | .338 |
| New York Yankees | 68 | 23 | 32 | 2 | 14 | .471 |
| Philadelphia Athletics | 63 | 19 | 28 | 8 | 22 | .444 |
| St. Louis Browns | 61 | 17 | 26 | 9 | 26 | .426 |
| Washington Senators | 63 | 16 | 24 | 3 | 13 | .381 |
| **Totals** | **456** | **135** | **185** | **37** | **120** | **.406** |

# The .400 Club

A list of .400 hitters since the 1900 season. The .400 mark was reached 22 times prior to 1900, including 11 in 1897. Tip O'Neill of St. Louis of the American Association holds the record for the highest average in a season at .485, that coming in 1887. Overall, the .400 mark has been achieved 35 times through the 2009 season.

| AVERAGE | PLAYER | YEAR | TEAM | LEAGUE |
| --- | --- | --- | --- | --- |
| .426 | Nap Lajoie | 1901 | Philadelphia | AL |
| .424 | Rogers Hornsby | 1924 | St. Louis | NL |
| .420 | George Sisler | 1922 | St. Louis | AL |
| .420 | Ty Cobb | 1911 | Detroit | AL |
| .409 | Ty Cobb | 1912 | Detroit | AL |
| .408 | Joe Jackson | 1911 | Cleveland | AL |
| .407 | George Sisler | 1920 | St. Louis | AL |
| **.406** | **Ted Williams** | **1941** | **Boston** | **AL** |
| .403 | Rogers Hornsby | 1925 | St. Louis | NL |
| .403 | Harry Heilman | 1923 | Detroit | AL |
| .401 | Rogers Hornsby | 1922 | St. Louis | NL |
| .401 | Bill Terry | 1930 | New York | NL |
| .401 | Ty Cobb | 1922 | Detroit | AL |

PLAYERS' MEMORIES

## CHAPTER 5

# The Players Remember Ted & Joe

The following former Major League Baseball players took the time to share their memories of Joe DiMaggio and Ted Williams. Their narratives follow. Because these interviews took place from January 2008 to June 2009, six players have since passed away. The author would like to remember those players:

DOM DIMAGGIO (1917-2009)

DON GUTTERIDGE (1912-2008)

SID HUDSON (1915-2008)

GEORGE KELL (1922-2009)

LES MCCRABB (1914-2008)

MICKEY VERNON (1918-2008)

PLAYERS' MEMORIES

# Yogi Berra

Full name: Lawrence Peter Berra

Born: May 12, 1925, St. Louis, MO

Died: Still talking baseball as of March 10, 2010.

Teams: Yankees (1946-63)
       Mets (1965)

Position: Catcher, outfielder

Bat/throw: Left/right; Height/weight: 5-8/194

All-star: 18 times; Most Valuable Player: 1951, 1954, 1955

Hall of Fame: Class of 1972 (second ballot, 85.6% of the vote)

CAREER PLAYING STATISTICS

Average: .285

Games: 2,120; At-bats: 7,555

Runs: 1,175; Hits: 2,150

Doubles: 321; Triples: 49

Home runs: 358; Runs-batted-in: 1,430

Base-on-balls: 704; Strikeouts: 414

On-base pct.: .338; Slugging pct.: .482

MANAGERIAL RECORD

Team: Yankees, 1964, 1984, 1985
    Wins: 192; Losses: 148; AL pennants: 1

Team: Mets 1972-75
    Wins: 292; Losses: 296; NL pennants: 1

FYI: Berra appeared in a record 14 World Series and was on the winning side 10 times, also a major league mark. He caught Don Larsen's no-hitter in the 1956 World Series, the only no-hitter in Series history through 2009. He later managed the Yankees (1964) and the Mets (1973) to pennants. It was midway through the 1973 season when his Mets were in last place in the National League East when Berra coined the phrase, "It ain't over till it's over." Considered a "bad-ball" hitter, Berra hit a career-high .322 in 1950. He picked up his nickname from a friend, Bobby Hofman, who said he resembled a Hindu holy man (yogi) they had seen in a movie. He served in the U.S. Navy during World War II. He was a "gunner's mate" in the D-

Three future Hall of Famers strike a pose: Ted Williams (left), Yogi Berra (center) and Mickey Mantle.

Day invasion. He is quite active with his "Yogi Berra Museum and Learning Center" on the campus of Montclair (N.J.) State University.

**YOGI SAID:**

"When I made it to the big leagues in 1946, I wasn't intimidated by Joe or Ted. I was just glad to be with the Yankees."

"Both of them were great and always treated me well. Nobody was more loyal, generous, courageous, more respected than Ted. He sacrificed his life and career for his country."

"Ted always said there was no one he admired, respected and envied more than Joe. They had tremendous respect for each other. They just went out and played their game. They were very close. They always complimented each other."

"I do remember when I was a rookie, Joe made an immediate impression on me. He pulled me aside my rookie year and said you always run out pop-ups because you're a Yankee and that's what a Yankee does."

"All Joe had to do was show up to make the Yankee clubhouse, the Yankee dugout and Yankee Stadium a better place. He was 'The Yankee Clipper,' the best player I ever saw."

"When I was catching, I tried to intimidate hitters by brushing dirt on their shoes. I did it for the heck of it, to get the hitter's attention. Ted always got mad at me because I'd try to carry on a conversation with him while he was trying to concentrate on hitting. Ted loved fishing, so I'd try to distract him about that, asking him questions about any recent big catches. I'd ask him where we was planning to eat that night. I'd do anything to try and distract him. He'd finally turn and look down at me and say, 'Will you shut up Yogi? I'm trying to hit.'"

"Of all the pitchers I caught, (teammate and lefty) Whitey (Ford) had the best luck against Ted. In Boston, with Ted being a left-handed hitter, we'd go in and out on him because of the big wall in left and that short right-field line. At Yankee Stadium, because he liked to pull the ball and we had that short porch in right, we'd pitch away from him. Ted had some problems with pitches low and away. Whitey's control gave him fits."

"Ted loved to talk about hitting. It was a science to him. He'd keep you all day talking about hitting, especially at the Hall of Fame induction ceremonies every year. If someone mentioned hitting, he'd keep you there for hours."

"Joe, on the other hand, was a different type of hitter than Ted. He was very selective and was more of a line-drive hitter than Ted. Joe may have had a keener eye, but Ted had more power."

"Joe was a great guy. My wife (Carmen) loved him. We'd go out to dinner a lot with Joe and Marilyn Monroe. Boy, she was something. Joe never let me pick up a check. Joe had a lot friends. If I picked the check up, he'd say he'd never go out with me again."

"Joe was just a quiet person, in the dressing room and on the field. He'd sit in the corner of the locker room, cross his legs and smoke a cigarette before and after a game. You'd walk by him and say 'hi.' Sometimes you got a response."

"Ted was more relaxed than Joe. If Joe didn't know you, he didn't want anything to do with you. Ted would talk to anyone."

"On the field, Joe was all business. He never walked to the out field. He always sprinted to center field. We didn't have a captain, but all of us followed Joe. He made all of us better players and a better team."

"Joe was a great outfielder, better than Ted. Whenever he'd yell at the other outfielders to get out of his way, they got out of his way. He covered a lot of ground in center at Yankee Stadium. Ted had that short left field at Fenway (in Boston)."

"Personality-wise, Joe and Ted were very different. Joe was never booed by the fans. He was also courteous with the press. Ted had run-ins with the press in Boston and the fans really got on him."

"Joe would go out at night, while Ted was usually in bed by 10."

**.406 or 56?** "That's a tough one. Let's just say I would have liked to have had both players on my team. Joe was the better fielder and base runner, and a great hitter. Ted was the better hitter, though. I don't think either mark will be broken. I don't see any .400 hitters out there and I just don't see anyone hitting in 56 straight games."

PLAYERS' MEMORIES

# Dom DiMaggio

Full name: Dominic Paul DiMaggio

Born: Feb. 12, 1917, San Francisco

Died: May 8, 2009, Marion, MA

Team: Red Sox (1940-42; 1946-53)

Position: Center field

Bat/throw: Right/right; Height/weight: 5-9/168

All-star: 7 times; Most Valuable Player: No

Hall of Fame: No

CAREER PLAYING STATISTICS

Average: .298

Games: 1,399; At-bats: 5,640

Runs: 1,046; Hits: 1,680

Doubles: 308; Triples: 57

Home runs: 87; Runs-batted-in: 618

Base-on-balls: 750; Strikeouts: 571

On-base pct.: .383; Slugging pct.: .419

FYI: DiMaggio batted .300 or better five times during his 11-season career. He ranked among the top 10 in the American League in runs scored, hits, doubles, stolen bases and times-on-base seven times. He was nicknamed "The Little Professor" because of his glasses and studious appearance. In 1949, he had a team-record 34-game hitting streak, which was ended, ironically, by a spectacular catch by his brother, Joe, on Aug. 9. In his later years, he said he "watched the stock ticker on television all day and Red Sox games all night." His other brother, Vince, was also a center fielder and played 10 seasons with the Braves, Reds, Pirates, Athletics and Giants. He was a .249 career hitter. Vince (1912-86) was the oldest of the three center-field brothers, followed by Joe (1914-99) and Dom (1917-2009).

**DOM SAID:**

"Even though he was my brother, we still had a rivalry. I played for the Red Sox, he played for the Yankees. It doesn't get much better than that, does it?"

Joe with his two brothers, Vince (left) and Dominic (right). All three played in the major leagues. Dominic was a standout centerfielder for the Red Sox.

"During the off-seasons, we got together a lot like any brothers. We were very close and talked about hitting quite a bit. During the season, though, he seldom spoke to me when we crossed paths. I was playing for the Yankees' main rivals during the 1940s."

"I remember Joe's hitting streak in 1941 quite well. When we were playing in Boston at Fenway Park, the guys in the left-field scoreboard would listen to the Yankee games on the radio to keep up with Joe. Whenever Joe got his hit to keep the streak alive, the guys in the scoreboard would yell out at Ted, who would then yell over to me in center field, 'Hey, Dommie, Joe got a hit.' Ted always kept me up-to-date."

"Joe was a leader, a quiet leader. The Yankees looked up to him. I looked up to him. He just didn't show a lot of emotion. I wasn't an overly emotional person myself, but I would say I was friendly with everyone."

"I was very close with Ted, Johnny (Pesky) and Bobby (Doerr). They all liked Joe, especially Ted. He loved the way Joe carried himself on and off the field. Joe was very business-like. Ted, who was always one of the guys, was one of the few players or managers who could get Joe to laugh."

"One thing that sticks out in my mind is for the first couple of years of his career, Ted would run out to left field with his hat raised above his head. He did this whenever he hit a homer. The fans loved it."

"As far as I'm concerned, Ted was and still is the best left-handed hitter, and Joe was and still is the best right-handed hitter. I do believe Joe was unhappy over the fact that he never hit .400 and Ted did (in 1941). Overall, though, I think Joe had the edge because of his overall play - defense, running the bases. I'm not saying that because he was my brother. That's just the way I saw it."

"Another thing about Ted that should tell fans something about him: In 1959 he made $120,000. When he met with team officials about his 1960 contract, they offered him another $120,000. Ted said no, that he didn't earn his 1959 salary (.254 average, 10 homers, 43 RBIs). He told the Red Sox he'd play the 1960 season for $90,000. How many players today would do something like that? I don't think any."

**.406 or 56?** "I think Ted's .406 average and Joe's 56-game hitting streak are equally great feats. If I have to pick one, I'd go with Joe's 56-gamer. To get a hit in 56 straight games is unthinkable. Will there be another .400 hitter or will someone break Joe's record? I don't know, but I've always believed that all records are made to be broken."

PLAYERS' MEMORIES

# Bobby Doerr

..............................................................

Full name: Robert Pershing Doerr

Born: April 7, 1918, Los Angeles, CA

Died: Still talking baseball as of March 10, 2010

Team: Red Sox (1937-44; 1946-51)

Position: Second base

Bat/throw: Right/right; Height/weight: 5-11/175

All-star: 9 times; Most Valuable Player: No

Hall of Fame: Class of 1986 by the veterans' committee


CAREER PLAYING STATISTICS

Average: .288

Games: 1,865; At-bats: 7,093

Runs: 1,094; Hits: 2,042

Red Sox teammates Bobby Doerr (left) and Johnny Pesky (right) were two of Ted's best friends. They remained best friends until Ted's death in 2002.

Doubles: 381; Triples: 89

Home runs: 223; Runs-batted-in: 1,247

Base-on-balls: 809; Strikeouts: 608

On-base pct.: .362; Slugging pct.: .461

FYI: Although he finished third in the 1946 MVP voting behind teammate Williams and Yankee pitcher Hal Newhouser, Babe Ruth called Doerr "the league's MVP, not Williams." Doerr drove in 116 runs and scored 95 times while hitting .271 as the Red Sox captured the AL pennant before losing to the

St. Louis Cardinals in seven games in the 1946 World Series. Doerr posted a .409 batting average in his only Series. A .980 fielder, he participated in 1,507 double-plays. He ranked among the top 10 in runs-batted-in eight times. As of March 1, 2010, he was the oldest living member (91) in the Hall of Fame. He held Red Sox team records in games, at-bats, hits, total bases and RBIs until his teammate and best friend, Williams, broke all those marks. He simply called Williams "9," Ted's uniform number.

**BOBBY SAID:**

"Ted lived and breathed hitting. He'd get (teammate and pitcher) Joe Dobson to throw to him when the stadium was empty and he'd hit for 30 minutes. I kept telling him he'd wear himself out. And Joe nearly pitched a full game out there throwing to Ted."

"Ted was the best hitter, but DiMaggio was the perfect player. He threw, ran, hit and made everything look easy. He could accelerate as good as anyone I've seen. He could go from first to third on a single better than anyone I saw."

"Joe also played in the toughest stadium (Yankee) in the American League. He had so much ground to cover in center field. Because most of the games were played during the day, Joe had to contend with the tough afternoon shadows at Yankee Stadium and all those white shirts in the bleachers."

"Ted, Babe Ruth, Lou Gehrig...... I'd take Joe over anyone of them. He was quiet, but you could sense his confidence. His teammates gained that confidence and inspiration from Joe. That's why the Yankees had all those great clubs. My gosh, look at Joe's record (13 seasons, 10 World Series, nine championships). We (the Red Sox) got into just one Series, 1946 against the Cardinals, and lost in seven games."

"Some people believed we lost to the Cardinals because of the shift they'd go to whenever Ted came up. They loaded up the right side (of the infield). The Cardinals' third baseman (Whitey Kurowski) played behind second base. Ted was a little stubborn and refused to hit to left field because he didn't want to swing at pitches outside the strike zone. He said he didn't want to develop bad habits. He had a bad Series, though, hitting .200 or something like that (.200 is correct). He felt terrible about that, but he believed there'd be more chances in future World Series. He never got there, though."

"Ted was a talker. He was friendly with all the players. I always got a kick out of the fact that another member of our team would hit a home run to win a game, but Ted would get the headlines because he beat out a bunt for a single. Ted sold newspapers. He didn't get along with the newspaper guys after his first couple of seasons. There were times when he'd spit in the direction of the writers in the press box. I'm not sure why because Ted was such a friendly character. All you had to do was say hello to him and he'd pull you aside and talk for 10 to 20 minutes."

"Another thing, whenever Joe or Ted took batting practice, the whole stadium came to a complete halt. All the fans and even the players stopped what they were doing to watch."

"Probably the thing I remember the most about Ted the player, besides his .406, was his two-out, three-run homer in the bottom of the ninth inning in the 1941 All-Star Game (in Detroit). It led us to a 7-5 win over the National League. Ted looked like a little kid running around the bases, clapping his hands, laughing and smiling. It was quite a sight."

**.406 or 56?** "Both are great accomplishments, but I think it would be harder to hit in 56 straight games. I do believe you won't see another .400 hitter or see anyone come close to DiMaggio's record because of the way relief pitching is today. In today's game, a batter might see as many as three or four different pitchers. Back in our days, we'd see the starting pitcher at least three times."

PLAYERS' MEMORIES

# Bob Feller

Full name: Robert William Andrew Feller

Born: Nov. 3, 1918, Van Meter, IA

Died: Still talking baseball as of March 10, 2010

Teams: Indians (1936-41; 1945-56)

Position: Pitcher

Bat/throw: Right/right; Height/weight: 6-0/185

All-star: 8 times; Most Valuable Player: No

Hall of Fame: Class of 1962
(first ballot; 93.8 percent of the vote)

CAREER PLAYING STATISTICS

Victories: 266; Losses: 162

Earned-run-average: 3.25

Games: 570; Games started: 484

Complete games: 279; Innings pitched: 3,827

Hits allowed: 3,271; Strikeouts: 2,581

Base-on-balls: 1,764; Home runs allowed: 224

FYI: Feller won the Triple Crown for pitchers in 1940 with 27 victories, a 2.61 ERA and 261 strikeouts. He led the American League in victories six times and in strikeouts seven (a career-high 348 in 1946). He was nicknamed "Rapid Robert" for his 100 mph fastball, as well as "The Heater from Van Meter." Growing up on a farm, his family built a "field of dreams" baseball field, complete with a scoreboard and stands. It is here where he learned the game. Feller signed with the Indians at the age of 17 for $1 and an autographed baseball. In one of his earliest starts, he struck out 17 batters. He and the Indians won the 1948 World Series in six games over the Boston Braves. Feller, however, lost both of his starts, the opener by a 1-0 count. He pitched three no-hitters and 12 one-hitters. He's the only pitcher to hurl a no-hitter on opening day, that coming in 1940 against the White Sox. He was the first pro baseball player to enlist in the armed services (Navy) the day after Japan attacked Pearl Harbor on Dec. 7, 1941, volunteering immediately for combat service. A Gun Captain on the *USS Alabama*, Feller missed four full seasons. He was awarded eight battle stars. The "Bob Feller Museum" in Van Meter opened in 1995.

For Hall-of-Fame pitcher Bob Feller (right), Joe (left) "was the toughest hitter" he ever faced.

## BOB SAID:

"Joe was a great hitter, had a great arm and was a good base runner, but Ted was the better hitter."

"When Ted came up (to the majors in 1939), we had heard a lot about him when he was in the minors, so we were looking for him. Ted was strictly a low-ball hitter his rookie year.

> "FOR ME, JOE WAS THE TOUGHEST HITTER. YOU HAD TO KEEP THE BALL AWAY FROM HIM."

He had very quick and strong wrists and, after a year, learned how to hit the high ball. Ted eventually became a good curveball hitter, too. Joe didn't like sinkerball pitchers and sliders, but he could handle the curve. Both could get around on the fastball, especially Ted."

"For me, Joe was the toughest hitter. You had to keep the ball away from him."

"Overall, Joe was the better player, too. Defensively, he had much better range and quickness and a more-accurate arm than Ted. Joe also got a good jump on the ball."

"Williams did a good job playing that Green Monster and short left field at Fenway, but away from Fenway he wasn't very good as a fielder."

"I had a much better relationship with Ted, who was a very generous player in many ways. Joe was a very private individual and was tight with money. Ted was one of my best friends on Earth. He was a great American."

"Neither one of them were good family men, though. A good family man is a good husband. Both had problems in that area."

"Joe was a bit intimidating to the writers, but was basically a nice guy to them. The Boston papers had a field day with Ted. They had maybe as many as 20 papers in Boston back then and all the reporters had to find something different to write about. Some stories were true, some weren't, but it bugged Ted day and night. It never affected his ability to hit, though."

**.406 or 56?** "You have to go with the 56-game hitting streak. I don't see anyone matching that mark. Ted's .406 might be broken because they change the rules so much these days."

## PLAYERS' MEMORIES

# Whitey Ford

Full name: Edward Charles Ford

Born: Oct. 21, 1928, New York, NY

Died: Still talking baseball as of March 10, 2010

Teams: Yankees (1950; 1953-67)

Position: Pitcher

Bat/throw: Left/left; Height/weight: 5-10/181

All-star: 12 times; Most Valuable Player: No

Hall of Fame: Class of 1974
(second ballot; 77.8 percent of the vote)

CAREER PLAYING STATISTICS

Victories: 236; Losses: 106.

Earned-run-average: 2.75.

Games: 498; Games started: 438.

Yankee pitcher Whitey Ford said the best way to try to get Ted (above) out was to mix up pitches. Ted was a little vulnerable with pitches low and away.

Complete games: 156; Innings pitched: 3,170.1.

Hits allowed: 2,766; Strikeouts: 1,956.

Base-on-balls: 1,086; Home runs allowed: 228.

FYI: Ford won numerous pitcher-of-the-year awards, including the Cy Young Award in 1961 when he went 25-4 and led the Yankees to the American League pennant. Nicknamed the "Chairman of the Board" by his Yankee teammates, Whitey's favorite "on-the-town" buddies were Billy Martin and Mickey Mantle. Ford ranked among the top 10 in victories per season and ERA 11 times during his 16-season career, and 10 times ranked among the leaders in strikeouts. He posted a 10-8 won-loss record and 2.71 ERA in 11 World Series, six of which the Yankees won. In 1963, he was third in the Most Valuable Player Award vote behind teammate Elston Howard and Detroit's Al Kaline.

**WHITEY SAID:**

"Both Joe and Ted were excellent. Ted was one of the best hitters in the game. Joe was the better overall player because of his defense and base running."

"Pitching to Ted, you just had to mix things up. He had no weakness. I simply threw what (catcher) Yogi (Berra) called because he knew all the hitters real well. You don't get a batter out on a certain pitch. You mix it up. You keep the hitter off-balanced."

"I'll never forget my debut (July 1, 1950) at Fenway Park. I got on the mound and I looked out at center field and I couldn't believe that Joe, a guy I idolized, was the centerfielder. (Ford only lasted a couple of innings as he allowed seven Boston runs)."

"I'll never forget how Mickey (Mantle) and I were scared to death to speak to Joe at first. Joe was a good guy. He had a lot of class. He hung out with good people and was a great dresser. He never hung out with us, though, at night. He was older than we were. He didn't associate with those of us who went out at night, guys like Billy (Martin) and Mickey."

"I played golf with both Joe and Ted a few times. Ted also took me fishing in Florida quite a few times. We became pretty close friends. We loved each other's company. I liked Ted as a person very much."

"And I really liked Joe. He was shy. I actually got to know him better after we both got out of baseball."

**.406 or 56?** "It's tough for a pitcher to pick the greater achievement. I don't think anyone will hit .400 again and I don't think anyone will hit in 56 straight games. They're equally impressive."

## PLAYERS' MEMORIES

# Don Gutteridge

........................................................

Full name: Donald Joseph Gutteridge

Born: June 19, 1912, Pittsburg, KS

Died: Sept. 7, 2008, Pittsburg, KS

Teams: Cardinals (1936-40)
Browns (1942-45)
Red Sox (1946-47)
Pirates (1948)

Position: Second, third, short

Bat/throw: Right/right; Height/weight: 5-8/165

All-star: No; Most Valuable Player: No

Hall of Fame: No

## CAREER PLAYING STATISTICS

Average: .256

Games: 1,151; At-bats: 4,202.

Runs: 586; Hits: 1,075.

Doubles: 200; Triples: 64.

Home runs: 39; Runs-batted-in: 391.

Base-on-balls: 309; Strikeouts: 444.

On-base pct.: .308; Slugging pct.: .362.

FYI: Don ranked among the top 10 in the American League twice in runs scored, and four times in triples and stolen bases. He appeared in two World Series: 1944 with the Browns and 1946 with the Red Sox. On both occasions, his teams lost to the Cardinals. In his second major league game, he collected six hits, an inside-the-park home run and stole home twice. He coached for the White Sox (1955-66 and 1968), then succeeded Hall-of-Famer and good friend Al Lopez as manager in 1969. He posted a 109-172 record before being dismissed with 26 games remaining in the 1970 season. When he died at the age of 96, he was the last-living member of the Boston Braves' 1944 World Series team.

## DON SAID:

"Ted and Joe had tremendous respect for each other. They pushed each other. They wanted to be better than the other. I know Ted and Joe checked the box scores every day to see how each other did."

"Ted was a great teammate when I was with the Red Sox (1946-47). I don't think there's ever been anyone who loved the game of baseball more than Ted."

"Ted was a player's buddy. He tried to help everyone with their hitting. Ted gave me some tips and made me a better hitter. He taught me discipline at the plate. Joe, on the other hand, was a loner. He didn't have a lot to say. You'd say hello to him and he'd act as though you weren't even there. He was always focused on the game, from the time he arrived at the park until an hour or so after the game."

"Overall, though, Joe had the edge on Ted. Joe was a better fielder, had a better arm and he could run the bases. Ted was the better hitter, though, but not a great left-fielder. He'd talked about hitting nonstop. There were times when he'd talk about hitting for an hour."

"Both players played on some great teams, but it seemed the Yankees always won in the 1940s and that was due to Joe's quiet leadership. Joe made all the Yankees better players. Ted made his teammates better hitters. Those Yankee teams of the 1940s were Hall of Famers, but I honestly believe the best team of the 1940s were the 1946 Red Sox. Thing is, Joe won a bunch (nine) of World Series and Ted got to play in just one. I think that really bothered Ted."

"We ran away with the (1946) pennant (12 games over Detroit and 17 over the Yankees) and played St. Louis in the World Series. We had everything going for us. We clinched the pennant early and were rested, while the Cardinals were forced into a best-of-three playoff with Brooklyn (which the Cards won in two games). We lost in the Series in seven games. We probably would have won the Series had Ted gotten three or four more base hits. He had a terrible World Series (5-for-25 for a .200 average with one run-batted in)."

"Everyone likes to blame (Johnny) Pesky for 'holding the ball' as (Enos) Slaughter scored the winning run from first base in Game 7. Pesky didn't hold the ball. He was nothing more than a scapegoat. We just didn't get the production from Ted at the plate that we were expecting. I don't know how many runners he left in scoring position. Ted insisted on pulling the ball to the right side instead of trying to go to the opposite field. The Cardinals went with the defense devised by Cleveland where they would stack the right side of the infield so Ted couldn't get a ball through for a single."

"Joe was a clutch player, especially during the World Series. It seemed every time the Yankees needed a big hit, Joe got it." (DiMaggio had a .271 average in 10 World Series).

**.406 or 56?** "Both were great achievements and the fact they took place in the same year is really unbelievable, but I think Ted's .406 tops the 56-game streak because it was over an entire season. I know both felt a tremendous amount of pressure. To hit safely in 56 straight games will never be topped. And I don't think today's ballplayer has the ability to get four hits every 10 times at-bat."

## PLAYERS' MEMORIES

# Ralph Houk

Full name: Ralph George Houk

Born: Aug. 9, 1919, Lawrence, KS

Died: Still talking baseball as of March 10, 2010

Teams: Yankees (1947-54)

Position: Catcher

Bat/throw: Right/right; Height/weight: 5-11/193

All-star: No; Most Valuable Player: No

Hall of Fame: No

CAREER PLAYING STATISTICS

Average: .272

Games: 91; At-bats: 158

Runs: 12; Hits: 43

Doubles: 6; Triples: 1

Home runs: 0; Runs-batted-in: 20

Base-on-balls: 12; Strikeouts: 10

On-base pct.: .327; Slugging pct.: .323

MANAGERIAL RECORD

Team:  Yankees, 1961-63, 1966-73
          Wins: 944; Losses: 806; AL pennants: 3
          World Series titles: 2.

Team:  Tigers, 1974-78
          Wins: 363; Losses: 443

Team:  Red Sox, 1981-84
          Wins: 312; Losses: 282

FYI: Houk won five World Series rings—two as a player (1947 and 1952), two as the Yankees' manager in 1961 and 1962, and one as a member in the front office of the 1987 Twins. As a player, he spent his career playing behind Yankee catcher Yogi Berra. A major—thus the nickname "The Major"—in the Army during World War II, he was a combat veteran of Bastogne and the Battle of the Bulge. He was awarded a Silver Star, Bronze Star and Purple Heart. He managed the Yankees in 1961 during the great home run chase between Roger Maris and Mickey Mantle. Maris finished with 61 in 162 games to break Babe Ruth's 154-game mark of 60. Mantle finished with 54. As a manager, one of his trademarks was kicking his cap when arguing with an umpire. He was considered a "player's manager." Mantle once said of Houk: "He brought out the best in everybody, and that included me. I consider myself lucky to have played for him." Houk also spent many seasons in the Yankees' front office.

**RALPH SAID:**

"The thing that always stood out to me was the great friendship Ted and Joe had. They had a very good relationship and always got along well. There was no rivalry. Of course, whenever the Red Sox and Yankees played, the photographers always wanted to get photos of the two together. They'd spend a lot of time joking with each other."

"As a player, I was with Joe a lot. He was a leader without talking. He was all business. He'd come into the dressing room, get a cup of coffee, read the paper and go over that day's opposing pitcher. Probably no player was more prepared for a game and pitcher than Joe."

"As a hitter, Joe never chased a bad ball (28.4 strikeouts per season). And no one was better going from first to third on a hit. Defensively, he could get to balls in the outfield you'd think he didn't have a chance to get, but he'd glide to the balls."

"Ted was a solid fielder. He played that left field wall (at Fenway) well. And as a hitter, he was very selective. I don't think he ever swung at a ball out of the strike zone. The umpires had to be on their toes whenever Ted came to the plate. We tried to get him out with pitches low and away, but didn't have much success."

**.406 or 56?** "That's a tough decision to make. Both had great eyes and it's tough to compare them. Both were great accomplishments, but I think it's harder to hit in 56 straight. I was lucky to play with Joe, know Ted and manage players like Yogi (Berra), Mickey (Mantle), Roger (Maris) and Yaz (Carl Yastrzemski of the Red Sox). But I give the nod to Joe."

# PLAYERS' MEMORIES

# Sid Hudson

Full name: Sidney Charles Hudson

Born: Jan. 3, 1915, Coalfield, TN

Died: Oct. 10, 2008; Waco, TX

Teams: Senators (1940-42; 1946-52)
   Red Sox (1952-54)

Position: Pitcher

Bat/throw: Right/right; Height/weight: 6-4/180

All-star: Two times; Most Valuable Player: No

Hall of Fame: No


CAREER PLAYING STATISTICS

Victories: 104; Losses: 152

Earned-run-average: 4.28

Games: 380; Games started: 279

Complete games: 123; Innings pitched: 2,181

Hits allowed: 2,384; Strikeouts: 734

Base-on-balls: 835; Home runs allowed: 136

FYI: Hudson won 17 games as a rookie, a career high. A workhorse, he ranked among the top 10 in the American League in innings pitched and complete games four times. When he retired, he became a scout and an assistant coach with the Senators and Rangers. He was also the pitching coach at Baylor University (1987-93).

**SID SAID:**

"Even though we were on different teams, Ted and I became pretty good friends."

"I remember we went golfing in Florida one day. Both of us weren't any good. We came to a hole where you had to hit the ball over a lake and then over a tree to get to the green. A good golfer didn't have a problem clearing both. Well, I played it safe and hit my ball to the left to avoid the water. Ted stepped up to the tee and hit a high one into the air. He got excited because he thought he was going to clear the lake and the tree, but the ball fell in the water. He pulled out another ball and hit. Same thing. He pulled out a third ball. Again in the water. I thought he was going to explode, he was that angry. He was quite a cursor. Ted could really swear. He finally took a fourth ball and threw it over the lake and tree. It landed on the green."

"Ted had a lot of enemies with the sports writers and it was just his nature to curse during interviews. Joe probably never uttered a single curse word. He was so calm and cool. Nothing seemed to rattle him. The Yankee press and fans loved Joe. The Boston media and fans really got on Ted's nerves. When he came out and said he'd rather play for the Yankees, there was an uproar in Boston. That's when all of his problems started dealing with the writers and fans. But when he returned from serving his country, everybody seemed to get along better."

"Ted was a real friendly guy with the players. He'd come over to the visiting team's dressing room and talk about hitting, fishing and hunting. You didn't see Joe do that. He was very reserved. He had a quiet confidence. His teammates got along with Joe. Joe led by example. That's why the Yankees won so many pennants and World Series with Joe. I remember reading in the papers that Joe had hinted that he won team championships and that Ted won individual awards. That didn't sit well with Ted."

**.406 or 56?** "I think there will be another .400 hitter someday. I don't see anyone hitting in 56 straight games, so I'll go with DiMaggio's record."

PLAYERS' MEMORIES

# George Kell

Full name: George Clyde Kell

Born: Aug. 23, 1922; Swifton, ARK

Died: March 24, 2009; Swifton, ARK

Teams: Athletics (1943-46)
Tigers (1946-52)
Red Sox (1952-54)
White Sox (1954-56)
Orioles (1956-57)

Position: Third

Bat/throw: Right/right; Height/weight: 5-9/175

All-star: 10 times; Most Valuable Player: No

Hall of Fame: Class of 1983 (veterans' committee)

George Kell of Detroit had a close relationship with Joe (left), shown with rookie Mickey Mantle in 1951.

## CAREER PLAYING STATISTICS

Average: .306

Games: 1,795; At-bats: 6,702

Runs: 881; Hits: 2,054

Doubles: 385; Triples: 50

Home runs: 78; Runs-batted-in: 870

Base-on-balls: 621; Strikeouts: 287

On-base pct.: .367; Slugging pct.: .414

FYI: Kell ranked among the top 10 in batting average eight times, including 1949 when he won the hitting crown with a .343 mark. He batted above .300 eight consecutive seasons. He led the league in hits and doubles twice (1950 and 1951). He was tough to strike out, going down once every 23.4 at-bats in his career. He turned to the broadcast booth for 40 seasons.

**GEORGE SAID:**

"Ted was a great hitter, but not a great outfielder. He didn't pretend to be a great outfielder. He wasn't a liability, but he was in the lineup to hit and he was the best hitter I have ever seen. He kind of lumbered around in left."

"I was much closer with Ted because I played with him for a few years (1952-54). Joe and I were good friends. He was a loner, but he and I talked a lot. I think he looked for someone to talk baseball with and that person happened to be me."

"I remember Joe didn't grant too many interviews, but after I retired, I did the CBS Game of the Week in 1958 with Dizzy Dean. Joe agreed to an interview with me as long as we kept the conversation to baseball. At the time, there was a lot of talk about his family life and his marriage (to Marilyn Monroe), so I honored that and we talked baseball. Lots of writers bothered him for quotes about Marilyn. He said, 'I'll be glad to be on your show, but keep it to baseball.'"

"Joe was a very literate man, very smart. He set the tone in the Yankee locker room, that sense of professionalism which helped them to so many championships."

"I'll never forget my first all-star game (in 1947 in Chicago). I was pretty nervous before the game. Joe came over and sat next to me and said, 'Go out there and play like you do everyday.' That had a calming effect on me."

"Ted could be pretty moody at times. He wasn't real pleasant to be around when he went hitless in a game. Boy, he could swear, but he always treated me nice. Many times when he wasn't married, he'd invite me over to his house and he'd cook steaks for us in his backyard."

"I remember one day when he got back from Korea, he brought a rifle into the locker room and called all of us over to his locker. He took the rifle apart and put it back together in less than five minutes. He was really proud of that."

"Ted took that rifle and started shooting pigeons at Fenway Park one off-day. Fenway was full of pigeons and Ted was shooting them down. He got into a lot of trouble, but he didn't seem to mind. He thought he was helping out the Red Sox and their fans."

"I also remember when I beat him out for the 1949 batting championship (.34291 to Ted's .34276) when I was with the

Tigers. I went 2-for-3 on the last day of the season and Ted went 0-for-3. It cost Ted the Triple Crown (43 homers and 159 RBIs). If I had one less hit or one more at-bat, Ted would have won the batting title. On the other hand, if Ted had one more hit or one less at-bat, he would have won. The next spring, some photographers wanted to take a picture of the No. 1 and No. 2 hitters from the previous season. Ted would have none of that. He said I won the batting championship and that I deserved the credit. He said he didn't belong in the picture."

"The best player? I'd take Joe. He could do everything Ted could do, but a little better. He ran the bases better and played great defense."

"The GREATEST player I ever saw, though, was Mickey Mantle. He could hit the ball further than Ted or Joe. He could steal bases, bunt, run and he was superb in center field, right and left."

**.406 or 56?** "I think Joe's 56-game hitting streak was a greater achievement than Ted's .406 average. Joe put it on the line everyday. He had to get a hit everyday. I think people forget that. I don't think anyone will ever hit in 56 consecutive games again. Will someone hit .400? Yes, I think someday someone will. George Brett (of Kansas City) came close (in 1980) when he entered the last couple of weeks of the season in the .390s, but he finished at .390."

## PLAYERS' MEMORIES

# Les McCrabb

Full name: Lester William McCrabb

Born: Nov. 4, 1914; Wakefield, PA

Died: Oct. 8, 2008, Wakefield, PA

Teams: Athletics (1939-42; 1950)

Position: Pitcher

Bat/throw: Right/right; Height/weight: 5-11/175

All-star: No; Most Valuable Player: No

Hall of Fame: No

CAREER PLAYING STATISTICS

Victories: 10; Losses: 15

Earned-run-average: 5.96

Games: 38; Games started: 27

Complete games: 13; Innings pitched: 210

Hits allowed: 270; Strikeouts: 57

Base-on-balls: 63; Home runs allowed: 24

FYI: McCrabb only appeared in 38 major league games during his five-season career. He did manage a 9-13 record and 11 complete games in 1941 for the last-place Athletics (64-90). He retired after the 1942 season, then made a comeback in 1950 at the age of 35. He appeared in only two games in 1950 and had an ERA of 27.00 before being released.

**LES SAID:**

"The 1941 season was really the only full season I pitched for the Athletics, but I got a good taste of both Ted and Joe. Ted hit three homers off me that season, while Joe went 0-for-7. That's my claim to fame. I got Joe out on high sliders. I had a crummy curveball."

"I always got a kick out of Ted because he always played umpire. If the count was 3-0 or 3-1 and the umpire called ball 4, Ted would stand there in the batter's box and stare down the umpire. Ted didn't want to walk. He wanted to hit. He'd simply drop his bat and slowly walk down to first base."

"I was in Philadelphia that final day of the 1941 season when Ted played both ends of the double-header to push his average above the .400 mark. He went 6-for-8 in the two games. It was a thrill to watch. I was 26 and until 1941 didn't have much of a taste of the major leagues. (Philadelphia manager) Connie Mack really didn't give me much of a chance."

> "I ALWAYS GOT A KICK OUT OF TED BECAUSE HE ALWAYS PLAYED UMPIRE."

**.406 or 56?** "I think there will be another .400 hitter someday. I don't see anyone hitting in 56 straight games, so I'll go with DiMaggio's record."

## PLAYERS' MEMORIES

# John "Les" Moss

Full name: John Lester Moss

Born: May 14, 1925; Tulsa, OK

Died: Still talking baseball as of March 10, 2010

Teams: Browns (1946-50)
       Red Sox (1951)
       Browns (1951-53)
       Orioles (1954-55)
       White Sox (1955-58)

Position: Catcher

Bat/throw: Right/right; Height/weight: 5-11/205

All-star: No; Most Valuable Player: No

Hall of Fame: No

## CAREER PLAYING STATISTICS

Average: .247

Games: 824; At-bats: 2,234

Runs: 210; Hits: 552

Doubles: 75; Triples: 4

Home runs: 63; Runs-batted-in: 276

Base-on-balls: 282; Strikeouts: 316

On-base pct.: .333; Slugging pct.: .369

FYI: Moss spent most of his career serving as a backup catcher —twice to Sherman Lollar with the Browns and the White Sox. He started only 120 games in his career. He did hit above .290 twice. He managed two teams: the 1968 White Sox (12-24) when skipper Al Lopez became ill and the 1979 Tigers (27-26). He was fired as the Tigers' manager a third of the way through the 1979 season and was replaced by Sparky Anderson.

## JOHN SAID:

"Ted was born to hit. We tried everything in the world on him, but nothing worked. He was a little vulnerable in the lower, outside corner, but he still connected and got his hits. He was by far the toughest hitter. He shared his hitting knowledge, too. If someone was in a slump, Ted would work with that player, he was that kind of guy."

"DiMaggio was a great hitter, too, but Ted was better. We had some luck with Joe by feeding him the hard sliders, but that's when he was getting older in the late 1940s. During his prime, you couldn't get him out, period."

"Defensively, Joe was head and shoulders above Williams. Joe made all the hard plays look easy. Williams kind of roamed around out there in left field. He didn't have the speed or quickness that Joe had."

"Joe also had better players around him. Those Yankee teams during the 1940s were so dominant. Their bench was so strong, the Yankees could have probably fielded two separate teams that were better than most of the teams in baseball."

"Joe was quiet and reserved. Ted was loud and outgoing."

**.406 or 56?** "Both are great achievements that will never be matched. No one has come close to either mark. I don't want to choose between the two, they're both that great."

## PLAYERS' MEMORIES

# Johnny Pesky

..............................................................

Full name: John Michael Pesky

Born: Sept. 27, 1919; Portland, OR

Died: Still talking baseball as of March 10, 2010

Teams: Red Sox (1942; 1946-52)
      Tigers (1952-54)
      Senators (1954)

Position: Shortstop, third base

Bat/throw: Left/right; Height/weight: 5-9/168

All-star: Once; Most Valuable Player: No

Hall of Fame: No

CAREER PLAYING STATISTICS

Average: .307

Games: 1,270; At-bats: 4,745

Runs: 867; Hits: 1,455

Doubles: 226; Triples: 50

Home runs: 17; Runs-batted-in: 404

Base-on-balls: 662; Strikeouts: 218

On-base pct.: .307; Slugging pct.: .394

FYI: Pesky was the first player in MLB history to collect more than 200 hits in his first three seasons. He teamed with second baseman Bobby Doerr to form one of the game's greatest double-play combinations. He batted above .300 five times and exceeded the 100-run mark six. He ranked among the top 10 in on-base percentage six times. His uniform No. 6 has been retired by the Red Sox. He is also a member of the Red Sox's Hall of Fame. The right-field foul pole at Fenway Park is called "The Pesky Pole" because he won a game for pitcher Mel Parnell with a homer that hit the right-field pole. He missed three full seasons (1943-45) serving in the Navy during World War II.

**JOHNNY SAID:**

"Williams was the best hitter, but Joe was the complete player. Ted was just known for his hitting, whereas Joe had a great arm and was strong and could hit the ball a long way. Joe wasn't a big home run hitter (369), but Ted (521) was. Williams was complete, but he couldn't run like Joe and play defense like Joe. Ted hit .400, Joe didn't. I think that bugged Joe a little. I played with Ted everyday for 10 years and I couldn't have played with anyone better."

"Joe was very quiet. His brother and my teammate, Dom, was more outgoing than Joe. On the other hand, Ted was very friendly with everyone. He laughed a lot and loved talking about hitting. Believe me, I know. We spent a lot of time together eating before and after the games—myself, Ted, Dom and Bobby (Doerr)."

"Ted used to joke around with me about my real last name — Paveskovich. He called it a disease. And with my long, pointy nose, Ted called me 'needle nose.' I loved that guy."

"Ted spent a lot of time taking batting practice. Everyone got four minutes in the (batting) cage. Ted got six to seven minutes. Ted just understood hitting and he knew the pitchers. He loved Bob Feller (of Cleveland). He thought Bob was the best pitcher in the game."

"When Williams took batting practice, especially on the road, everyone would stop and watch. Even the players. He'd also get very impatient with the guy hitting in front of him, telling him to hurry up and get out of the batting cage."

"Toward the end of his career, Joe became friendlier. We'd joke with one another quite a bit. He was a fine man. After we retired, we went to dinner once and I had a chance to meet his wife, Marilyn Monroe. What a beautiful person. You couldn't help liking Joe."

> "WHAT A BEAUTIFUL PERSON. YOU COULDN'T HELP LIKING JOE."

"There was one day when I didn't like Joe that much, though. In a game in Boston, Joe knocked me down on my ass to break up a doubleplay. It was a clean play, but I didn't like it. About a week later we were playing at Yankee Stadium and Joe was on first base with one out. I told Bobby (Doerr) that if the batter, Tommy Henrich, hit the ball to him, I wanted the ball quickly because I wanted to hit Joe between the eyes with my throw to first. I hit him in the shoulder instead. Joe looked at me and said, 'Now we're even. I nearly killed you in Boston last week.'"

"I know for a fact that it bothered Ted he never won a World Series or appeared in just one (1946). He had a terrible Series, but he got us there. After we lost the seventh game (to the Cardinals), Ted sat in front of his locker and cried. I'll never forget that. He felt like he let the team down. That one World

Series appearance really bothered him to the day he died."

"When we were done playing, all of us (Williams, Doerr and Dom) remained close. I remember the last time I saw Ted before he died in Florida. Dom and I visited him. He was happy to see us, but you could tell he was running out of time. I just wanted to cry."

**.406 or 56?** Joe's 56-game streak was great, but it doesn't top Ted's .406. That's a greater accomplishment. No one will hit .400 again."

## PLAYERS' MEMORIES

# Billy Pierce

Full name: Walter William Pierce

Born: April 2, 1927; Detroit, MI

Died: Still talking baseball as of March 10, 2010

Teams: Tigers (1945, 1948)
      White Sox (1949-61)
      Giants (1962-64).

Position: Pitcher

Bat/throw: Left/left; Height/weight: 5-10/160

All-star: 7 times; Most Valuable Player: No

Hall of Fame: No

### CAREER PLAYING STATISTICS

Victories: 211; Losses: 169

Earned-run-average: 3.27

Games: 585; Games started: 432

Complete games: 193; Innings pitched: 3,306.2

Hits allowed: 2,989; Strikeouts: 1,999

Base-on-balls: 1,178; Home runs allowed: 284

FYI: Pierce earned 186 of his 211 career wins with the White Sox. He was named The Sporting News' American League Pitcher of the Year in 1956 and 1957, when he posted 20-9 and 20-12 records, respectively. His 1.97 ERA in 1955 led all AL pitchers. He also led the AL in complete games from 1956 to 1958 with 21, 16 and 19. He ranked among the top 10 in AL pitching victories and ERA seven times. Pierce appeared in two World Series, both losing efforts—the 1959 White Sox vs. the Dodgers and the 1962 Giants vs. the Yankees. He did post a 1-1 record in Series play with a 1.89 ERA. In a three-game National League playoff against the Dodgers in 1962, he hurled a three-hit shutout and a save.

**BILLY SAID:**

"The greatest hitter? Ted Williams. The greatest all-around player? Joe DiMaggio. Joe was such a great fielder, base runner and hitter. I remember my first year in the majors and the first time I pitched against Joe. He swung and hit a 3-0 pitch that is still probably going somewhere."

"Joe was such a great clutch player and great leader for the Yankees. I think that's why the Yankees won all those championships during his career (9 out of 10). Defensively, he covered so much ground at Yankee Stadium, both in left-center and right-center. Center fielders catch so many of a pitcher's mistakes. They help out in left-center and right-center. Joe had such a terrific arm, too. If someone singled to center with a runner on second, Joe would usually get that base runner at home plate."

"Ted played the wall at Fenway in Boston well. If a ball was hit to left, a runner on second would have to stop at third because Ted knew that wall so well, the caroms and rebounds. Compared to Joe, though, he had less ground to cover."

"I had to pitch carefully to both of them. You tried not to let them beat you. Both could get around on a fastball pretty easily. Being a lefty, I had a little more luck with Ted than I did with Joe, who could absolutely kill a fastball."

"Ted got a lot of bad press in Boston. Why? I don't know. He was loved by all the players. He would talk to everybody, especially about hitting. He even talked about hitting with opposing players, giving them tips. And he knew the pitchers so well. It was like he knew what pitch was coming."

"Joe was more reserved. You would be lucky to get a 'hi' from him, but I would have loved to have had him on my team."

"Ted was a very determined hitter. If you made him look bad on a swing, he'd grab his cap and pull it down tighter. I faced a lot of great hitters, but I don't know of anybody who was better."

"Ted was the only guy I knew, who, when he came up to bat, players and fans wouldn't get up to use the restroom. They didn't want to miss the opportunity to see Williams hit. You could say the same thing about Joe. When Ted or Joe were in town, the stadiums were packed."

**.406 or 56?** "To get a hit every single day with nine fielders out there is fantastic, but to hit .400, that's four clean hits every 10 at-bats. That's fantastic, too. I guess I'd give a slight edge to Joe's 56-game streak. Look at all the pitchers he faced."

## PLAYERS' MEMORIES

# Eddie Robinson

Full name: William Edward Robinson

Born: Dec. 15, 1920; Paris, TX

Died: Still talking baseball as of March 10, 2010

Teams: Indians (1942, 1946-48)
      Senators (1949-50)
      White Sox (1950-52)
      Athletics (1953)
      Yankees (1954-56)
      Athletics (1956)
      Tigers, Indians and Orioles (1957)

Position: First base

Bat/throw: Left/right; Height/weight: 6-1/210

All-star: 4 times; Most Valuable Player: No

Hall of Fame: No

## CAREER PLAYING STATISTICS

Average: .268

Games: 1,315; At-bats: 4,282

Runs: 546; Hits: 1,146

Doubles: 172; Triples: 24

Home runs: 172; Runs-batted-in: 723

Base-on-balls: 521; Strikeouts: 359

On-base pct.: .353; Slugging pct.: .440

FYI: Robinson's best overall season came in 1951 when he batted .282, hit 29 homers and drove home 117 runs for the White Sox. The previous season he batted a career-high .313. His .990 career fielding percentage is among the best for first basemen. He also participated in 1,018 double-plays, including 143 and 145 in 1951-52, respectively. He played a big role in the Indians' 1948 six-game World Series win over the Boston Braves, hitting .300.

### EDDIE SAID:

"DiMaggio was the better overall player and had a better overall game, but Williams was a better hitter. Joe was a tremendous center fielder, while Ted was a good left fielder. Nothing special. He didn't have too much ground to cover in left at Fenway."

"As a team player, Joe was the whole ball of wax, a hell of a team leader. That's why the Yankees won all those pennants and World Series. The Yankees followed Joe. They looked up to him and admired his professionalism."

"To this day I have never seen anyone play center better than Joe. It was unbelievable watching him chase down balls in right and left center field. I think people overlooked his speed as a defensive player. He got such a tremendous jump on the ball. Today, a lot of those same hits fall in for doubles or triples."

"One thing that sticks in my mind is batting practice. Whenever Joe or Ted were in the (batting) cage, the whole stadium came to a standstill. I know I never missed the opportunity to watch them take batting practice. They just tore the cover off the balls."

"Ted was and still is the greatest hitter. It was a science to him. He knew the pitchers. I think he knew exactly what pitch was coming. They say he could see the red stitches on the ball. That's tough when a pitcher is throwing you 85 to 95 mph fastballs."

**.406 or 56?** "It's hard to compare the two. I think they're equally impressive and important. You really have to give Ted all the credit in the world the way he got that .406 on the last day of the 1941 season. He could have sat out that last day, but he insisted on playing that double-header (against Philadelphia) and he got six hits. A 56-game hitting streak is unbelievable and I don't think that mark will ever be broken. There might be another .400 hitter one day, so I give a slight edge to Joe."

"AS A TEAM PLAYER, JOE WAS THE WHOLE BALL OF WAX, A HELL OF A TEAM LEADER."

## PLAYERS' MEMORIES

# Al Rosen

Full name: Albert Leonard Rosen

Born: Feb. 29, 1924; Spartanburg, SC

Died: Still talking baseball as of March 10, 2010

Teams: Indians (1947-56)

Position: Third base

Bat/throw: Right/right; Height/weight: 5-10/180

All-star: 4 times; Most Valuable Player: 1953

Hall of Fame: No

CAREER PLAYING STATISTICS

Average: .285

Games: 1,044; At-bats: 3,725

Runs: 603; Hits: 1,063

Out of respect, Al Rosen of Cleveland always called Joe (above) "Mr. DiMaggio."

Doubles: 165; Triples: 20

Home runs: 192; Runs-batted-in: 717

Base-on-balls: 587; Strikeouts: 385

On-base pct.: .384; Slugging pct.: .495

FYI: Rosen averaged only 12.7 errors per season at the hot corner for the Tribe. His finest season came in 1953 when the American League's MVP batted .336 with league-highs in homers (43) and runs-batted-in (145). He missed winning the Triple Crown that season, finishing .001 points behind batting champion Mickey Vernon of the Senators. He was annually among the league leaders in several key offensive categories, including slugging percentage, on-base percentage and runs-batted-in. He is one of the greatest Jewish players to play the game, along with Hank Greenberg and Sandy Koufax. He appeared in two World Series: 1948 when the Indians beat the Braves and 1954 when the Tribe lost to the Giants. He often challenged any player to a fight if that player slurred his religion.

**AL SAID:**

"I always called Joe 'Mr. DiMaggio' out of respect. I came up in 1947 toward the end of Joe's career, so my perspective of the two really starts in 1947-50 when Joe was in and out of the lineup because of injuries and the Yankees were feeding (Mickey) Mantle for center field."

"I remember we played an afternoon game at Yankee Stadium late in September (17, 1951). Bob Lemon was pitching for us. DiMaggio was on third. I walked over to Joe and said, 'Mr. DiMaggio, do you think Phil (Rizzuto) is going to bunt.' Joe said, 'Sure he is.' I told him I would charge on every play. Joe just smiled at me. Well, Phil laid down the bunt and Joe scored the winning run, which clinched the American League pennant for the Yankees. Lemon was so furious that he threw his glove up into press box behind home plate."

"Williams was the type of player who had everyone's attention when he took batting practice. All the players would get there early to see Ted take batting practice and the beauty of his swing."

"In 1951, Ted broke his collarbone. Now Ted was always very nice to me, so I went to see him in the hospital. At that time he was wearing a cast that made him look like a chicken. When he saw me, he said 'You're not hitting.' He threw a pillow at me. He gave me a long lecture about hitting. Well, that night I went out and hit a home run to beat the White Sox. The next day, I went back to see him, but he wouldn't let me in the room. He was just horsing around, but while he was helping me, he didn't want me to hurt his club with swinging a hot bat."

**.406 or 56?** "Ted was the best hitter, but Joe was the best overall player. Ted's .406 and Joe's 56-game hitting streak were both absolutely superb performances. I don't see anyone reaching those milestones in my lifetime. It just won't happen. I don't see any Williams or DiMaggios out there. There may be another .400 hitter out there, but I don't see anyone hitting in 56 straight games, so I guess I'll vote for Joe. One thing to remember is both players had great players hitting in front of them, which gave them the opportunity to drive in all those runs. The Yankees and Red Sox had great teams during the 1940s. Except for 1946 (Red Sox) and 1948 (Indians), the Yankees won five AL pennants and four World Series."

## PLAYERS' MEMORIES

# Carl Scheib

Full name: Carl Alvin Scheib

Born: Jan. 1, 1927; Gratz, PA

Died: Still talking baseball as of March 10, 2010

Teams: Athletics (1943-45; 1947-54)
Cardinals (1954)

Position: Pitcher

Bat/throw: Right/right; Height/weight: 6-1/192

All-star: No; Most Valuable Player: No

Hall of Fame: No

CAREER PLAYING STATISTICS

Victories: 45; Losses: 65

Earned-run-average: 4.88

Games: 267; Games started: 107

Complete games: 47; Innings pitched: 1,066

Hits allowed: 1,124; Strikeouts: 290

Base-on-balls: 493; Home runs allowed: 99

FYI: At the age of 16, Scheib was the youngest player in the American League in 1943 as well as in 1944. His best season came in 1948 when he had a record of 14-8 with a 3.94 ERA and 15 complete games. He was one of the game's top hitting pitchers, posting a career average of .250 with five homers and 55 RBIs.

**CARL SAID:**

"If I were starting a team, I'd pick Ted Williams. Not just because he was the greatest hitter, but because of his personality. He was just a wonderful guy. He was fun to be with. You could kid around with him. If you said something to Ted, he'd stop and talk and talk your ear off. Joe, who I didn't know very well, kept to himself. He was high society. He made the nightclub scene at night when he wasn't in his room."

"I remember I made a start in Boston during the 1946 season and I got Ted out three straight times with curveballs. He sat on the bench fuming. He yelled out at me that the next time he came to bat he'd hit a home run. Sure enough, I threw him a curveball and he hit a two-run homer to beat me."

"We used to try and bug Ted when he came to the plate, too. Our catcher, Joe Tipton, used to get on Ted all the time, making him laugh. A lot of times, Ted had to step out of the batter's box."

"The only problem for Ted was his relationship with the press. Why? I don't know. I do know Ted would stop and sign some autographs, then leave. The press got on him for not signing for everyone."

"Now as an outfielder, Joe was greater than Ted, although Ted played that green wall (at Fenway) pretty well. With Joe, I've never seen anyone catch the ball and get rid of it any quicker. He prevented a lot of runs from scoring with that right arm of his. Those Yankee pitchers were lucky to have him in center. You don't see that anymore. The players today just don't have the arms. My gosh, today a runner on second base scores on a single to left field. And if the left fielder tries to throw the runner out at home, the throw is usually off target. There's no excuse for that."

**.406 or 56?** "Both are highly rated in my book, but I have to go with the .406 average. A guy who gets four hits every 10 at-bats gets my vote. I don't think anyone will hit .400 again, nor do I think anyone will ever hit in 56 straight games again. But, sorry Joe, Ted gets my vote."

## PLAYERS' MEMORIES

# Bobby Shantz

..........................................................

Full name: Robert Clayton Shantz

Born: Sept. 26, 1925; Pottstown, PA

Died: Still talking baseball as of March 10, 2010

Teams: Athletics (1949-56)
      Yankees (1957-60)
      Pirates (1961)
      Astros (1962)
      Cardinals (1962-64)
      Cubs (1964)
      Phillies (1964)

Position: Pitcher

Bat/throw: Right/left; Height/weight: 5-6/142

All-star: 3 times; Most Valuable Player: 1952

Hall of Fame: No

## CAREER PLAYING STATISTICS

Victories: 119; Losses: 99

Earned-run-average: 3.38

Games: 537; Games started: 171

Complete games: 78; Innings pitched: 1,935.2

Hits allowed: 1,795; Strikeouts: 1,072

Base-on-balls: 643; Home runs allowed: 151

FYI: Shantz took the American League by storm in his fourth season (1952) with the fourth-place Athletics, posting a 24-7 record, 27 complete games and an ERA of 2.48 to be named the league's Most Valuable Player. His 2.45 ERA in 1957 with the Yankees (11-5 record) was the league's lowest. An outstanding fielder (16 career errors in 16 seasons), Shantz won eight Gold Gloves. He was 0-1 in two World Series, both with the Yankees in 1957 and 1960, both seven-game losses to the Braves and Pirates, respectively. In the final inning of the 1952 All-Star Game, the side-armer struck out Whitey Lockman (.290 average), Jackie Robinson (.308) and Stan Musial (.336).

## BOBBY SAID:

"Did they tell me how to pitch to Ted? Yep. It was great advice. Encouraging. They said he had no weakness, wouldn't swing at a bad ball, has the best eyes in the business and can kill you with one swing. He won't hit anything bad, but don't give him anything good."

"That pretty much sums up pitching against Ted. You had to be very careful. You couldn't feed him fastballs, especially over the plate. You tried to get him to hit curveballs low and away."

"If I missed the plate by a quarter of an inch, Ted would take it. Some umpires were actually afraid to call balls and strikes against Ted because they thought Ted had a better eye than they did."

"Ted was the greatest hitter I ever faced. This might surprise a lot of people, but Joe wasn't the greatest right-handed hitter I ever faced. It was Roy Sievers (.267 career hitter from 1949-65). In 16 seasons, I think I got him out only a handful of times."

"Now DiMaggio was no slouch. He had that stretched stance and so much confidence. He was a damn-good hitter and a great guy. I went barnstorming with him in Japan one year and the people in Japan loved him. The Japanese people nearly tipped our car over when they swarmed the car. Joe and I had a good relationship because we spent time together."

"A lot of people say Joe was quiet, which he was, and stayed to himself, which he did, but if he got to know you and earned his trust he became your friend. Heck, I remember seeing him in the Yankee dressing room one day with a line of players seeking his autograph."

"Ted was outgoing. He never turned down a conversation, except with the sports writers, who wrote a lot of bad things about him. The Boston writers badgered him, always asking negative questions. The New York press understood Joe and almost treated him like royalty. If Joe felt like talking, the press would be there. If he didn't want to talk, the writers left him alone. Joe never had a problem with the writers or the fans."

**.406 or 56?** "I think it would be the toughest thing to get hits in 56 straight games. Hitting .406 was tough, too. Ted probably could have had a higher average had he taken advantage of that short left-field wall at Fenway, but he never did. He insisted on pulling everything. We stacked our defense on the right side of the field, but he'd still hit those darts past the players. If I had to give an edge to one of the two, I'd say DiMaggio because he was the better fielder. There were others I faced—Henry Aaron, Willie Mays, Yogi Berra, Mickey Mantle and Roberto Clemente, who was one of the better all-around players in the game. But if you put Mays in there with Joe and Ted, I'd say he (Mays) was the best player."

PLAYERS' MEMORIES

# Roy Sievers

..............................................................

Full name: Roy Edward Sievers

Born: Nov. 18, 1926; St. Louis, MO

Died: Still talking baseball as of March 10, 2010

Teams: Browns (1949-53)
 Senators (1954-59)
 White Sox (1960-61)
 Phillies (1962-64)
 Senators (1965)

Position: First base, outfield

Bat/throw: Right/right; Height/weight: 6-1/192

All-star: 7 times; Most Valuable Player: No

Hall of Fame: No

## CAREER PLAYING STATISTICS

Average: .267

Games: 1,887; At-bats: 6,387

Runs: 945; Hits: 1,703

Doubles: 292; Triples: 42

Home runs: 318; Runs-batted-in: 1,147

Base-on-balls: 841; Strikeouts: 920

On-base pct.: .354; Slugging pct.: .475

FYI: Sievers was the American League's Rookie of the Year in 1949 when he batted .306, hit 16 homers and drove home 91 runs for the Browns. Seven times he ranked among the top 10 in homers, runs-batted-in, extra-base hits, on-base percentage and slugging percentage. His 42 homers in 1957 led the American League. He finished third in the AL Most Valuable Player voting behind Mickey Mantle and Ted Williams.

**ROY SAID:**

"When it came to fielding and hitting together, I'd give the edge to DiMaggio. He was more of an all-around player. Thing is, he was a very private person. I'd say hello to him and he'd run right past you without saying a word. Joe also wouldn't sign many autographs. He was a tough autograph. I guess that's why people pay so much for one today on the internet and at card shows."

"Ted was the better hitter. He was a precision hitter. He never hit the ball to left, though. He always pulled the ball to right. He had 20-20 eyesight. Whenever a new pitcher came in, he knew that pitcher. He'd remember what that pitcher threw him the last time he batted against him."

"Defensively, Joe was by far the better player. He patrolled that big center field at Yankee Stadium. I remember one time a ball was hit toward right-center and (right fielder) Hank Bauer came over and caught it. Joe got upset, walked over to Bauer and said, 'That's my territory.'"

"Joe was great to watch in the field. He didn't make any mistakes during his career. And he had such a great arm. He was always ahead of the game. By that I mean he knew exactly what he'd do with the ball if it came to him."

"Ted was a good defensive player in left field at Fenway. I don't think he got enough credit for his defense. He knew every speck of that big, green wall."

"Although he talked a lot and joked around, Ted was actually straight-laced most of the time. He was always very good to me. You just had to be on his right side. He always said I had the second-best, right-handed swing in baseball. He ranked me just a shade below Joe."

"He was always talking to the Boston brass about trading for me. It never happened, which was disappointing. I would have loved to have played with Ted and the Red Sox and in the '46 World Series. I never played in a World Series. I came close in 1964 when I was with the Phillies, but late in the season was sold to Washington. I could have helped the Phillies get to the Series. Instead, they fell apart and St. Louis won the National League. But like Ted always said, it was just a thrill putting on a major league uniform."

"Ted had a great supporting cast during the 1940s, guys like Dom (DiMaggio), (Bobby) Doerr, Johnny (Pesky), (Joe) Cronin and a great pitching staff led by (Mel) Parnell, but except for 1946, they never had the momentum to overtake the Yankees. You have to credit DiMaggio for that. He was their quiet leader. He led by example, not by words."

**.406 or 56?** "Hey, I would have liked to have had both on my team. Both were great accomplishments, but I have to go with DiMaggio's 56. There were a couple of questionable calls that kept the streak going, but you can't go back and dissect every at-bat and hit. I don't think anyone will reach either achievement."

## PLAYERS' MEMORIES

# Virgil Trucks

..........................................................

Full name: Virgil Oliver Trucks

Born: April 26, 1917, Birmingham, AL

Died: Still talking baseball as of March 10, 2010

Teams: Tigers (1941-43; 1945-52)
　　　　Browns (1953)
　　　　White Sox (1953-55)
　　　　Tigers (1956)
　　　　Athletics (1957-58)
　　　　Yankees (1958)

Position: Pitcher

Bat/throw: Right/right; Height/weight: 5-11/198

All-star: 2 times; Most Valuable Player: No

Hall of Fame: No

## CAREER PLAYING STATISTICS

Victories: 177; Losses: 135

Earned-run-average: 3.39

Games: 517; Games started: 328

Complete games: 124; Innings pitched: 2,682

Hits allowed: 2,416; Strikeouts: 1,534

Base-on-balls: 1,088; Home runs allowed: 188

FYI: Trucks posted double-digit victories 11 times, including 1953 when he won 20 for the Browns (5 wins) and White Sox (15). He ranked among the top 10 in strikeouts-per-nine-innings 10 times. His 153 strikeouts in 1949 led the AL. Seven times he was among the top 10 in winning percentage. In 1952, he hurled two no-hitters, both 1-0 decisions against the Senators and the Yankees. In the Tigers' 1945 World Series win over the Cubs, he pitched a complete-game, 4-1 victory in Game 2. He committed just 27 errors in 17 seasons.

**VIRGIL SAID:**

"Without a doubt, Ted Williams was the toughest and greatest hitter I ever saw. There was no real way to pitch to him. He had such fantastic eyesight that he could see a fly on the center-field wall 400 feet away. No one pitch gave him a problem. I had a little luck with him with my slider, being a right-handed pitcher and Ted being a left-handed hitter. He loved fastballs, though. And, boy, did he hate to walk. He wanted his swings and hits. He was the most-difficult out in baseball during that era."

"Joe was a great all-around player and one of the greatest outfielders I have ever seen. At the plate, Joe had that big-open stance. I tried to get him out with outside sliders. I'm not saying I had a lot of luck."

"Joe was strictly all business. Very quiet. He was his own man. He was the Yankee leader. He helped Mickey Mantle. Mantle once told me Joe helped him the year after he retired (1951). Joe probably could have played another four years if it hadn't been for the spur on his heel. He still had great reflexes and his leadership in the Yankee dressing room was so valuable."

**.406 or 56?** "Both are great accomplishments that will probably never be duplicated. I admired both so much. Being a pitcher and wanting the runs, I'd have to give the nod to Ted's .406 because he got four hits every 10 times he batted, and that's a lot of runs (Ted's 1,839 RBIs to Joe's 1,537). There were others who I think deserve mentioning, guys like Mantle, and (Yankee catchers) Bill Dickey and Yogi (Berra). They were great players, too."

## PLAYERS' MEMORIES

# Mickey Vernon

Full name: James Barton Vernon

Born: April 22, 1918; Marcus Hook, PA

Died: Sept. 24, 2008; Media PA

Teams: Senators (1939-43; 1946-48)
      Indians (1949-50)
      Senators (1950-55)
      Red Sox (1956-57)
      Indians (1958)
      Braves (1959)
      Pirates (1960)

Position: First base.

Bat/throw: Left/left; Height/weight: 6-2/180

All-star: 7 times; Most Valuable Player: No

Hall of Fame: No

## CAREER PLAYING STATISTICS

Average: .286

Games: 2,409; At-bats: 8,731

Runs: 1,196; Hits: 2,495

Doubles: 490; Triples: 120

Home runs: 172; Runs-batted-in: 1,311

Base-on-balls: 955; Strikeouts: 869

On-base pct.: .359; Slugging pct.: .428

FYI: Vernon won a pair of batting crowns - .353 in 1946 and .337 in 1953. He ranked among the top 10 in runs-batted-in eight times and three times led the AL in doubles. He won a World Series ring with the Pirates, who beat the Yankees in seven games in 1960. Following his playing career, he managed the expansion Senators from 1961-63, posting a 135-227 record. He picked up the nickname "Mickey" as a child. In 2003 in Marcus Hook, PA., a bronze statue of Vernon was erected depicting his swing. When Vernon first saw it, he said: "When I played in Washington, all the statues around town showed men on horseback."

## MICKEY SAID:

"Probably my biggest thrill in baseball came in 1946 when I beat out Ted for the American League batting championship (.353 to .342). Of course, that season was his first back with Boston after three years at war, but I'll take it. Ted was nice about it. Who wouldn't be happy hitting .342?"

"In baseball, there's some talent and there's some luck involved. A ball dropping inches inside the foul line could have easily dropped inches outside. A bad-hop grounder that goes for a hit or a hit ball that just eludes the fielder, so all players, past and present, need a little luck. Of course, you have to hit the ball, which I think is the toughest thing to do in sports and there was no one better than Ted."

"DiMaggio was a great hitter, too, but Ted had the edge. Joe was by far the better fielder and base runner. And as quiet as he was, he was probably a better team leader than Ted. I think (Johnny) Pesky and (Bobby) Doerr and Joe's brother, Dom, were the Red Sox's leaders. Ted focused on hitting and playing the game to the best of his abilities every single game. When he came up to hit, believe me, every first baseman in the league took a couple of steps back because Ted could just hit the cover off the ball."

**.406 or 56?** "To hit in 56 straight games is probably one of the top two or three accomplishments in modern-day baseball. I think (Cincinnati pitcher) Johnny Vander Meer's back-to-back no hitters (in 1938) will never be duplicated, and I don't think anyone will ever hit in 56 straight. Think about the pressure DiMaggio faced every game during that streak. Ted's .406 average and the way he got it (the last day of the season) is an amazing story. If I have to pick, I'd have to go with Joe's 56 over Ted, as much as I loved that guy."

> "DIMAGGIO WAS A GREAT HITTER, TOO, BUT TED HAD THE EDGE."

### CHAPTER 6

# Joe Retires; Waits Three Years for Call From the Hall of Fame

In probably the biggest blunder in Hall of Fame voting, it took Joe DiMaggio three years to finally gain admission into baseball's highest and most-honored shrine.

From 1937 to 1945, there was no waiting period for players, managers and executives to be considered for the Hall in Cooperstown, N.Y. As a matter of fact, active players could be considered, as was the case with DiMaggio in 1945, six years before his retirement.

From 1946 through 1954, baseball installed a one-year waiting period. DiMaggio retired following the 1951 season, thus making him eligible for election in 1953.

Despite all of his greatness and achievements as a player, he managed a pitiful 44.5 percent of the vote (75 percent or higher is required) in 1953. In 1954, he gained 69.4 percent of the vote.

In 1953, pitcher Dizzy Dean, who won 150 games during a 12-year career with the Cardinals, Cubs and Browns; and outfielder Al Simmons of the Athletics, a 20-season veteran who hit a career .334 with 307 homers, were elected, along with six others from the late 1800s.

In 1954, Boston Braves shortstop Rabbit Maranville (82.9 percent), Yankee catcher Bill Dickey (80.2) and Giants first baseman Bill Terry (77.4) got the call.

Finally, the now-existing rule of a five-year waiting period was passed in 1954, but an exception was made for DiMaggio, who garnered 88.8 percent of the votes in 1955.

Why he wasn't elected in 1953 or 1954 is a mystery.

The Yankees tried to persuade DiMaggio to return for the 1952 season, offering him a fourth consecutive salary of $100,000, but he declined. At the age of 37, he simply said, "I no longer have it."

DiMaggio's announcement came on Dec. 11, 1951. He had hinted all season that 1951 would probably be his last.

"My mind was pretty much made up," he told the media.

Injuries also played a role in his decision. "My right knee kept buckling under me," he said. "Also both shoulders. These injuries have bothered me for a long time and finally retarded my swing so much I simply couldn't hit in front of the plate as I used to."

A .263 hitter in 1951, DiMaggio also said he would have made the same decision had he hit .350.

"I feel that I have reached the stage where I can no longer produce for my ball club, my manager, my teammates and my fans," DiMaggio said. "In closing, I feel I have been privileged to play all my major league baseball for the New York Yankees. It's been a privilege to play baseball at all."

> CASEY STENGEL, HIS MANAGER FOR THREE YEARS, SIMPLY SAID, "WHAT IS THERE TO SAY?"

"What I will remember most will be the great loyalty of the fans. They have been very good to me."

Casey Stengel, his manager for three years, simply said, "What is there to say?"

"I just gave the big guy's glove to the Hall of Fame, where Joe himself is certain to go. He was the greatest player I every managed. Right now, I still say there isn't another center fielder in baseball his equal."

Following DiMaggio's announcement, Ted Williams said he "would always be compared to Joe. We were the two top players in our league," he told *The Boston Globe*. "I always felt I was the better hitter, but I have to say he was the greatest player of our time. Joe even looked good striking out. He had a profound and lasting impact on this country."

Williams admitted that DiMaggio always had "more grace playing in the field."

Joe's replacement in center the following season for the Yankees? Future Hall of Famer Mickey Mantle.

On July 25, 1955, DiMaggio was inducted into the National Baseball Hall of Fame after receiving 223-of-251 votes (88.8 percent).

The following are excerpts of DiMaggio's Hall of Fame induction acceptance speech. The Hall of Fame, the New York Yankees, the Library of Congress and the official Joe DiMaggio website do not have a complete copy of his speech.

# Excerpts From Joe's Hall of Fame Speech

"Well, it's a strange feeling becoming a museum piece at the age of 40 …. if that's what they mean. But to the fellow who has made baseball his life's work, Cooperstown is more than a collection of relics and fancy-worded plaques. It is the final touch every major leaguer would like to add to his career. There is no greater honor."

"Now I've had everything except for the thrill of watching Babe Ruth play."

Yankee great and Hall-of-Famer Lou Gehrig (left) helped Joe (right) as a rookie.

"This is a happy day for me. It's a long step since that day 20 years ago when I was riding to St. Petersburg with (former Yankees) Tony Lazzeri and Frank Crosetti for my first spring training trip with the Yankees. They asked me to drive the last 200 miles and I said sheepishly, 'I don't drive.' I thought that was the end of my career."

"I watched every move Lou (Gehrig) made on and off the field. Also, I'd like to thank Joe McCarthy, my first major league manager, for the early training he gave me."

"The last chapter has been written. I can now close the book."

..................................

"NOW I'VE HAD

EVERYTHING EXCEPT

FOR THE THRILL

OF WATCHING

BABE RUTH PLAY."

..................................

## CHAPTER 7

# Ted Enters the Hall of Fame

On July 25, 1966, Ted Williams was inducted into Baseball's Hall of Fame in Cooperstown, N.Y. Unlike Joe DiMaggio, who mysteriously had to wait three years to enter the Hall, Williams was selected in his first year of eligibility, but received 282-out-of-302 votes, or 93 percent. It's hard to believe that 20 sports writers did not vote for the player whose accomplishments included the .406 batting average in 1941, two Triple Crowns, two Most Valuable Player Awards, six American League batting championships, 521 career home runs, a lifetime average of .344 and 21 All-Star Games. Of course, "Teddy Ballgame" did have plenty of run-ins with the media, so possibly those 20 took this as an opportunity to "get even" with the Red Sox star.

Many forget that Williams actually retired on Sept. 27, 1954, but he changed his mind on May 13, 1955 when his divorce from Doris Soule four days earlier became final. The court ordered Williams to pay Soule a $50,000 lump-sum payment, the $42,000 family house, full custody of their 7-year-old daughter, Barbara Joyce, $100 a month in child support and $125 in living expenses a month.

Williams, in need of money, signed a contract with the Red Sox for $60,000 to play the remainder of the season. When he did retire for good on Sept. 28, 1960, when he hit a home run in his very last at-bat, Williams said, "I must say my stay in Boston has been the most wonderful thing in my life. If I were ever asked what I would do if I had to start my baseball career over again, I'd say I would want to play in Boston for the greatest owner (Tom Yawkey) in the game and the greatest fans in America."

"They can talk about Babe Ruth and Ty Cobb and Rogers Hornsby and Lou Gehrig and Joe DiMaggio and Stan Musial," said Carl Yastrzemski, who replaced Williams in left field and produced a Hall of Fame career himself. "But I'm sure not one of them could hold cards and spades to Ted in his sheer knowledge of hitting. He studied hitting the way a stock broker studies the stock market."

"He taught me the fundamentals," Yaz said. "He taught me to swing only at good pitches. But about the time I became a sophomore in high school, he stopped. That probably helped me more than anything. Sometimes you have to work out things yourself."

Ted's rival and friend, DiMaggio, simply said, "Ted Williams is the greatest left-handed hitter I've seen." Asked again to access

Williams' career, DiMaggio repeated, "Ted Williams is the greatest left-handed hitter I've seen."

Also inducted that day was former New York Yankee Manager Casey Stengel, who managed the Yankees for 12 seasons (1949-60), won 10 American League pennants and seven World Series titles.

Ted joined the 500-Home-Run Club on June 17, 1960 in Cleveland where he connected off Indians pitcher Wynn Hawkins.

# Ted's Hall of Fame Acceptance Speech

"I guess every player thinks about going into the Hall of Fame. Now that the moment has come for me I find it difficult to say what is really in my heart. But I know it is the greatest thrill of my life."

"I received 280-odd votes from the writers. I know I didn't have 280-odd friends among the writers. I know they voted for me because they felt in their minds and in their hearts that I rated it, and I want to say to them: Thank you, from the bottom of my heart." (Williams actually received 282-of-302 votes, or 93.4 percent, the 18th highest percentage in Hall of Fame voting through 2009).

"Today I am thinking about a lot of things. I am thinking about my playground director in San Diego, Rodney Luscomb; my high school coach, Wos Caldwell; and my managers, who had so much patience with me—fellows like Frank Shellenback, Donie Bush, Joe Cronin and Joe McCarthy. I am thinking of Eddie Collins (who signed him), who had so much faith in me. To be in the Hall with him particularly, as well as those other great players, is a great honor. I'm sorry Eddie isn't here today."

"I'm thinking of Tom Yawkey. I have always said it: 'Tom Yawkey is the greatest owner in baseball.' I was lucky to have played on the club he owned, and I'm grateful to him for being here today."

"But I'd not be leveling if I left it at that. Ballplayers are not born great. They're not born great hitters or pitchers or managers, and luck isn't a big factor. No one has come up with a substitute for hard work. I've never met a great player who didn't have to work harder at learning to play ball than anything else he ever did. To me it was the greatest fun I ever had, which probably explains why today I feel both humility and pride, because God let me play the game and learn to be good at it."

"The other day Willie Mays hit his 522nd home run. He has gone past me, and he's pushing, and I say to him, 'Go get 'em Willie.'"

"Baseball gives every American boy a chance to excel. Not just to be as good as anybody else, but to be better. This is the nature of man and the name of the game. I hope some day Satchel Paige and Josh Gibson will be voted into the Hall of Fame as symbols of the great Negro players who are not here only because they weren't given the chance."

"As time goes on, I'll be thinking baseball, teaching baseball and arguing for baseball to keep it right on top of American sports, just as it is in Japan, Mexico, Venezuela and other Latin American and South American countries. I know Casey (Stengel) feels the same way."

"I also know I'll lose a dear friend if I don't stop talking. I'm eating into his time, and that is unforgivable. So in closing, I am grateful and know how lucky I was to have been born an American and had the chance to play the game I love, the greatest game."

# CHAPTER 8

# The Feud & 1949 Pennant Race

Ted Williams and Joe DiMaggio had a special relationship. They were close friends and had tremendous respect for one another. When Williams' Red Sox and DiMaggio's Yankees met, it wasn't unusual to see the two players together, laughing, talking about hitting and baseball. They brought out the best in each other.

Many times, Williams said there was no one he "admired, respected and envied more" than DiMaggio. Joe felt the same way about Ted.

In August 1949, however, the two friends got testy with one another, not face-to-face, but through the media.

With the two teams battling for the American League pennant, the Red Sox took two-of-three games at home on Aug. 9-11 against the Yankees. In the second game, the Yankees held a 3-2 lead when Williams launched a long drive to right-center. DiMaggio fielded the ball, "then looked up and saw Williams standing on second," the Yankee Clipper was quoted as saying in the *Boston Globe*. "I was stunned. I thought for sure he'd be resting at third," DiMaggio said.

The Boston press jumped on DiMaggio's quote, pointing out had Williams reached third, he could have scored on a sacrifice fly to tie the game at 3.

An annoyed Williams responded by telling the Boston press: "Nobody said anything when Joe DiMaggio failed to reach second when he hit the top of the left-field wall Tuesday night (a 6-3 Red Sox win). He settled for a single"

Williams' remark upset DiMaggio, who was quoted in the press as calling his friend a "crybaby."

The two did not speak to one another prior to the Thursday game at Fenway, a 7-6 Red Sox win. It wasn't until the Yankees moved on to Philadelphia for a five-game series when DiMaggio tried to clear the air with an apologetic statement.

"It looks like someone (the press) is trying to build up a situation that doesn't exist," he said. "It was an offhand remark. These things can get awfully mixed up if they are strung out."

Williams seemed happy with DiMaggio's comments, so "the feud" lasted approximately 48 hours. They had more-important matters to tend to.

Both players were leading their clubs into a dramatic September pennant race, which came down to the final two days of

Ted (left) and Joe (right) always had time to joke with one another.

the season at Yankee Stadium. Prior to play on Oct. 1, the Red Sox stood at 96-56, the Yankees 95-57. For the Yankees to win the pennant, they would have to win both games. The Red Sox needed one of the two.

DiMaggio often said that if his Yankees didn't win the American League title, he'd like to see the Red Sox take the crown. Besides Williams, DiMaggio had a lot of friends on the Red Sox, including his own fleshing blood, kid brother Dominic. "Dom" was three years younger than his brother and enjoyed a successful 11-year career as the Red Sox's center fielder.

The Yankees' Johnny Lindell settled the first game with an eighth-inning homer to power the New Yorkers to a 5-4 win and a tie for the American League pennant at 96-57.

On Oct. 2, the final day of the regular-season, the Yankees sent 20-game winner Vic Raschi against the Red Sox's Ellis Kinder, who was seeking his 24th victory. The two were locked in a masterful pitching duel until the eighth. With the Yankees leading, 1-0, Tommy Henrich homered, then Jerry Coleman drove in three with a base-loaded double for a 5-0 lead.

In the top of the ninth, the Red Sox made things interesting when Bobby Doerr drilled a two-run triple over DiMaggio's head in center field to make it 5-2.

Following Doerr's triple, DiMaggio, who appeared in and out of the Yankee lineup all season (73 games) due to a variety of injuries, called timeout. In dramatic fashion, he jogged from center, through the infield and into the Yankee dugout. DiMaggio's actions stunned the crowd, which gave him a standing ovation.

Later, DiMaggio said he should have caught Doerr's triple and that he was "unable to do my job."

"I had terrible pain in my shinbones," DiMaggio told the press. "I didn't want to fall on my face if another ball came my way."

The Yankees won, 5-3, and claimed the American League pennant by one game over the disappointed Red Sox. The year before, the Red Sox finished second after losing a one-game playoff to Cleveland.

DiMaggio finished his abbreviated season with a .346 batting average, while Williams hit .343 and 43 homers, drove in 159 runs and won his second Most Valuable Player Award. He missed winning a third Triple Crown by one hit or one base-on-ball. Batting champion George Kell of Detroit finished the season with a .34291 average, Williams .34276.

In the World Series, the Yankees took care of the Brooklyn Dodgers in five games. DiMaggio went 2-for-18 at the plate, a .111 average. It was actually a "punchless" Series, with the Dodgers hitting a team .210 and the Yankees .226.

For DiMaggio, the 1949 crown was his seventh of nine. For his friend Williams, he still had a big goose egg and he retired with it.

It was common to see Ted and Joe pose for photographs on the top step of the dugout.

# CHAPTER 9

# Ted & Joe Said It

## WORDS OF WISDOM FROM TED AND JOE:

"A person always doing his or her best becomes a natural leader, just by example." — Joe

"All managers are losers, they are the most expendable pieces of furniture on the face of the Earth." — Ted

"A ballplayer has to be kept hungry to become a big leaguer. That's why no boy from a rich family has ever made the big leagues." — Joe

"Baseball gives every American boy a chance to excel, not just to be as good as someone else, but to be better than someone else. This is the nature of man and the name of the game." — Ted

"All pitchers are born pitchers." — Joe

"God gets you to the plate, but once you're there, you're on your own." — Ted

"I'm just a ballplayer with one ambition, and that is to give all I've got to help my ball club win. I've never played any other way." — Joe

"A man has to have goals - for a day, for a lifetime - and that was mine, to have people say, 'There goes Ted Williams, the greatest hitter who ever lived.'" — Ted

"I think there are some players born to play ball." — Joe

"Baseball is the only field of endeavor where a man can succeed three times out of 10 and be considered a good performer." — Ted

"If anyone wants to know why three kids in one family made it to the big leagues, they just had to know how we helped each other and how much we practiced back then. We did it every minute we could." — Joe

"Baseball's future? Bigger and bigger, better and better! No question about it." — Ted

"Pair up in threes." — Joe

"By the time you know what to do, you're too old to do it." — Ted

"The phrase 'off with the crack of the bat', while romantic, is really meaningless, since the outfielder should be in motion

long before he hears the sound of the ball meeting the bat."
— Joe

"I hope somebody hits .400 soon. Then people can start pestering that guy with questions about the last guy to hit .400."
— Ted

"There is always some kid who may be seeing me for the first time. I owe him my best." — Joe

"There has always been a saying in baseball that you can't make a hitter, but I think you can improve a hitter. More than you can improve a fielder. More mistakes are made hitting than in any other part of the game." — Ted

"Too many kids today are playing major league ball and don't belong there."— Joe

"I've found that you don't need to wear a necktie if you can hit."— Ted

"When baseball is no longer fun, it's no longer a game."
—Joe

"If there was ever a man born to be a hitter, it was me."
— Ted

"You always get a special kick on opening day, no matter how many you go through. You look forward to it like a birthday party when you're a kid. You think something wonderful is going to happen." — Joe

"There's only one way to become a hitter. Go up to the plate and get mad. Get mad at yourself and mad at the pitcher." — Ted

# CHAPTER 10
# Ted & Joe by the Numbers

*A variety of statistics, comparisons and projections by Joe DiMaggio and Ted Williams.*

## CAREER STATS LOST TO THE WARS

One has to wonder what type of career statistics Ted Williams and Joe DiMaggio would have posted had they not lost playing time during their prime due to World War II and, for Williams, the Korean War.

Based on their career numbers, it's easy to project what type of numbers they would have posted. (next page)

*A variety of statistics, comparisons and projections by Joe DiMaggio and Ted Williams.*

# Joe

For example, DiMaggio missed three seasons (1943-45) because of WW II. By taking his per-season average statistics during his 13-year career, multiplying them by three and adding them to his career stats, DiMaggio's career numbers would have looked like this:

**PROJECTED NUMBERS**

**Average:** .325

hits: 2,725; home runs: 444; runs-batted-in: 1,892

**ACTUAL NUMBERS**

**Average:** .325

hits: 2,214; home runs: 361; runs-batted-in: 1,537

*Not taken into consideration in these projections for Ted and Joe are possible injuries and rained-out games that weren't made up.*

# Ted

Williams' career numbers would have also been even more impressive by using the same formula. He missed three seasons (1943-45) for World War II and large portions of two more (1952-53) for the Korean War. Since he played in only 43 games those two seasons, those statistics are eliminated from the equation. Multiply his average statistics by five, his career numbers would have looked like this:

## PROJECTED NUMBERS

**Average:** .344

hits: 3,352; home runs: 658; runs-batted-in: 2,323

## ACTUAL NUMBERS

**Average:** .344

hits: 2,654; home runs: 521; runs-batted-in: 1,839

# Ted & Joe Season-by-Season

## The season-by-season statistics of Joe DiMaggio (JD) and Ted Williams (TW)

\* LEAGUE LEADER
\*\*MOST VALUABLE PLAYER

| 1936 | G | AB | R | H | 2B | 3B | HR | RBI | SB | CS | BB | SO | BA | SALARY |
|---|---|---|---|---|---|---|---|---|---|---|---|---|---|---|
| JD | 138 | 637 | 132 | 206 | 44 | 15* | 29 | 125 | 4 | 0 | 24 | 39 | .323 | $8,500 |

| 1937 | G | AB | R | H | 2B | 3B | HR | RBI | SB | CS | BB | SO | BA | SALARY |
|---|---|---|---|---|---|---|---|---|---|---|---|---|---|---|
| JD | 151 | 621 | 151* | 215 | 35 | 15 | 46* | 167 | 3 | 0 | 64 | 37 | .346 | 17,000 |

| 1938 | G | AB | R | H | 2B | 3B | HR | RBI | SB | CS | BB | SO | BA | SALARY |
|---|---|---|---|---|---|---|---|---|---|---|---|---|---|---|
| JD | 145 | 599 | 129 | 194 | 32 | 13 | 32 | 140 | 6 | 1 | 59 | 21 | .324 | 25,000 |

| 1939 | G | AB | R | H | 2B | 3B | HR | RBI | SB | CS | BB | SO | BA | SALARY |
|---|---|---|---|---|---|---|---|---|---|---|---|---|---|---|
| JD** | 20 | 462 | 108 | 176 | 32 | 6 | 30 | 126 | 3 | 0 | 52 | 20 | .381* | 27,500 |
| TW | 149 | 565 | 131 | 185 | 44 | 11 | 31 | 145* | 2 | 1 | 107 | 64 | .327 | 6,500 |

| 1940 | G | AB | R | H | 2B | 3B | HR | RBI | SB | CS | BB | SO | BA | SALARY |
|---|---|---|---|---|---|---|---|---|---|---|---|---|---|---|
| JD | 132 | 508 | 93 | 179 | 28 | 9 | 31 | 133 | 1 | 2 | 61 | 30 | .352* | 32,500 |
| TW | 144 | 561 | 134* | 193 | 43 | 14 | 23 | 113 | 4 | 4 | 96 | 54 | .344 | 12,000 |

| 1941 | G | AB | R | H | 2B | 3B | HR | RBI | SB | CS | BB | SO | BA | SALARY |
|---|---|---|---|---|---|---|---|---|---|---|---|---|---|---|
| JD** | 139 | 541 | 122 | 193 | 43 | 11 | 30 | 125* | 4 | 2 | 76 | 13 | .357 | 37,500 |
| TW | 143 | 456 | 135* | 185 | 33 | 3 | 37* | 120 | 2 | 4 | 147* | 27 | .406* | 20,000 |

| 1942 | G | AB | R | H | 2B | 3B | HR | RBI | SB | CS | BB | SO | BA | SALARY |
|---|---|---|---|---|---|---|---|---|---|---|---|---|---|---|
| JD | 154 | 610 | 123 | 186 | 29 | 13 | 21 | 114 | 4 | 2 | 68 | 36 | .305 | 43,750 |
| TW | 150 | 522 | 141* | 186 | 34 | 5 | 36* | 137* | 3 | 2 | 145* | 51 | .356* | 35,000 |

| 1943 | G | AB | R | H | 2B | 3B | HR | RBI | SB | CS | BB | SO | BA | SALARY |
|---|---|---|---|---|---|---|---|---|---|---|---|---|---|---|
| JD | MILITARY | | | | | | | | | | | | | |
| TW | MILITARY | | | | | | | | | | | | | |

| 1944 | G | AB | R | H | 2B | 3B | HR | RBI | SB | CS | BB | SO | BA | SALARY |
|---|---|---|---|---|---|---|---|---|---|---|---|---|---|---|
| JD | MILITARY | | | | | | | | | | | | | |
| TW | MILITARY | | | | | | | | | | | | | |

| 1945 | G | AB | R | H | 2B | 3B | HR | RBI | SB | CS | BB | SO | BA | SALARY |
|---|---|---|---|---|---|---|---|---|---|---|---|---|---|---|
| JD | MILITARY | | | | | | | | | | | | | |
| TW | MILITARY | | | | | | | | | | | | | |

| 1946 | G | AB | R | H | 2B | 3B | HR | RBI | SB | CS | BB | SO | BA | SALARY |
|---|---|---|---|---|---|---|---|---|---|---|---|---|---|---|
| JD | 132 | 503 | 81 | 146 | 20 | 8 | 25 | 95 | 1 | 0 | 59 | 24 | .290 | 43,750 |
| TW** | 150 | 514 | 142* | 176 | 37 | 8 | 38 | 123 | 0 | 0 | 156* | 44 | .342 | 50,000 |

| 1947 | G | AB | R | H | 2B | 3B | HR | RBI | SB | CS | BB | SO | BA | SALARY |
|---|---|---|---|---|---|---|---|---|---|---|---|---|---|---|
| JD** | 141 | 534 | 97 | 168 | 31 | 10 | 20 | 97 | 3 | 0 | 64 | 32 | .315 | 43,750 |
| TW | 156 | 528 | 125* | 181 | 40 | 9 | 32* | 114* | 0 | 1 | 162* | 47 | .343* | 75,000 |

| 1948 | G | AB | R | H | 2B | 3B | HR | RBI | SB | CS | BB | SO | BA | SALARY |
|---|---|---|---|---|---|---|---|---|---|---|---|---|---|---|
| JD | 153 | 594 | 110 | 190 | 26 | 11 | 39* | 155* | 1 | 1 | 67 | 30 | .320 | 70,000 |
| TW | 137 | 509 | 124 | 188 | 44* | 3 | 25 | 127 | 4 | 0 | 126* | 41 | .369* | 90,000 |

| 1949 | G | AB | R | H | 2B | 3B | HR | RBI | SB | CS | BB | SO | BA | SALARY |
|---|---|---|---|---|---|---|---|---|---|---|---|---|---|---|
| JD | 76 | 272 | 58 | 94 | 14 | 6 | 14 | 67 | 0 | 1 | 55 | 18 | .346 | 100,000 |
| TW** | 155* | 566 | 150* | 194 | 39* | 3 | 43* | 159* | 1 | 1 | 162* | 48 | .343 | 100,000 |

| 1950 | G | AB | R | H | 2B | 3B | HR | RBI | SB | CS | BB | SO | BA | SALARY |
|---|---|---|---|---|---|---|---|---|---|---|---|---|---|---|
| JD | 139 | 525 | 114 | 158 | 33 | 10 | 32 | 122 | 0 | 0 | 80 | 33 | .301 | 100,000 |
| TW | 89 | 334 | 82 | 106 | 24 | 1 | 28 | 97 | 3 | 0 | 82 | 21 | .317 | 125,000 |

| 1951 | G | AB | R | H | 2B | 3B | HR | RBI | SB | CS | BB | SO | BA | SALARY |
|---|---|---|---|---|---|---|---|---|---|---|---|---|---|---|
| JD | 116 | 415 | 72 | 109 | 22 | 4 | 12 | 71 | 0 | 0 | 61 | 36 | .263 | 100,000 |
| TW | 148 | 531 | 109 | 169 | 28 | 4 | 30 | 126 | 1 | 1 | 144* | 45 | .318 | NA |

# TED WILLIAMS
# DURING THE POST-DiMAGGIO ERA

| YEAR | G | AB | R | H | 2B | 3B | HR | RBI | SB | CS | BB | SO | BA | SALARY |
|---|---|---|---|---|---|---|---|---|---|---|---|---|---|---|
| 1952 | 6 | 10 | 2 | 4 | 0 | 1 | 1 | 3 | 0 | 0 | 2 | 2 | .400 | NA |
| 1953 | 37 | 91 | 17 | 37 | 6 | 0 | 13 | 34 | 0 | 1 | 19 | 10 | .407 | NA |
| 1954 | 117 | 386 | 93 | 133 | 23 | 1 | 29 | 89 | 0 | 0 | 136* | 32 | .345 | NA |
| 1955 | 98 | 320 | 77 | 114 | 21 | 3 | 28 | 83 | 2 | 0 | 91 | 24 | .356 | 60,000 |
| 1956 | 136 | 400 | 71 | 138 | 28 | 2 | 24 | 82 | 0 | 0 | 102 | 39 | .345 | 125,000 |
| 1957 | 132 | 420 | 96 | 163 | 28 | 1 | 38 | 87 | 0 | 1 | 119 | 43 | .388* | 125,000 |
| 1958 | 129 | 411 | 81 | 135 | 23 | 2 | 26 | 85 | 1 | 0 | 98 | 49 | .328* | NA |
| 1959 | 103 | 272 | 32 | 69 | 15 | 0 | 10 | 43 | 0 | 0 | 52 | 27 | .254 | 125,000 |
| 1960 | 113 | 310 | 6 | 98 | 15 | 0 | 29 | 72 | 1 | 17 | 75 | 41 | .316 | 90,000 |

**TOTALS**

| | G | AB | R | H | 2B | 3B | HR | RBI | SB | CS | BB | SO | BA |
|---|---|---|---|---|---|---|---|---|---|---|---|---|---|
| JD | 1736 | 6821 | 1390 | 2214 | 389 | 131 | 361 | 1537 | 30 | 9 | 790 | 369 | .325 |
| TW | 2292 | 7706 | 1798 | 2654 | 525 | 71 | 521 | 1839 | 24 | 17 | 2021 | 709 | .344 |

## DiMAGGIO'S CAREER HIGHS (13 SEASONS)

| G | AB | R | H | 2B | 3B | HR | RBI | SB | CS | BB | SO | BA |
|---|---|---|---|---|---|---|---|---|---|---|---|---|
| 154 | 637 | 151 | 215 | 44 | 15 | 46 | 167 | 6 | 2 | 80 | 39 | .381 |

## TED WILLIAMS' CAREER HIGHS (19 SEASONS)

| G | AB | R | H | 2B | 3B | HR | RBI | SB | CS | BB | SO | BA |
|---|---|---|---|---|---|---|---|---|---|---|---|---|
| 156 | 566 | 150 | 194 | 44 | 14 | 43 | 159 | 4 | 4 | 162 | 64 | .406 |

## OTHER DiMAGGIO CAREER TOTALS

| | |
|---|---|
| ON-BASE PERCENTAGE: | .398 |
| SLUGGING PERCENTAGE: | .579 |
| GROUNDED INTO DOUBLE PLAYS: | 130 |

## OTHER WILLIAMS CAREER TOTALS

| | |
|---|---|
| ON-BASE PERCENTAGE: | .482 |
| SLUGGING PERCENTAGE: | .634 |
| GROUNDED INTO DOUBLE PLAYS: | 197 |

# Ted & Joe by the Average

*A look at the season average statistics of Joe DiMaggio and Ted Williams*

|  | DIMAGGIO | WILLIAMS |
|---|---|---|
| SEASONS | 13 | 19 |
| GAMES | 133.5 | 120.6 |
| AT-BATS | 524.7 | 405.6 |
| RUNS | 106.9 | 94.6 |
| HITS | 170.3 | 139.7 |
| DOUBLES | 29.9 | 27.6 |
| TRIPLES | 10.1 | 3.7 |
| HOME RUNS | 27.8 | 27.4 |
| RUNS-BATTED-IN | 118.2 | 96.8 |
| STRIKEOUTS | 28.4 | 37.3 |
| BASE-ON-BALLS | 60.8 | 106.4 |
| BATTING AVERAGE | .325 | .344 |
| ON-BASE PERCENTAGE | .398 | .482 |
| SLUGGING PERCENTAGE | .579 | .634 |
| TOTAL BASES | 303.7 | 257.1 |
| GROUNDED INTO DPS | 10.0 | 10.4 |
| PUTOUTS | 348.4 | 218.8 |
| ASSISTS | 11.8 | 7.5 |
| ERRORS | 8.1 | 5.9 |
| DOUBLE PLAYS | 2.3 | 1.6 |
| FIELDING PERCENTAGE | .978 | .974 |

# Joe's Yankees vs. Ted's Red Sox

*How DiMaggio's Yankees and Williams' Red Sox fared in head-to-head competition and in the standings*

| 1939 | W | L | GB | WORLD SERIES |
|---|---|---|---|---|
| 1ST YANKEES | 106 | 45 | - | YANKEES BEAT REDS, 4 GAMES TO 0 |
| 2ND RED SOX | 89 | 62 | 17 | (RED SOX WON SEASON SERIES, 11-8) |

| 1940 | W | L | GB | WORLD SERIES |
|---|---|---|---|---|
| 3RD YANKEES | 88 | 66 | 2 | REDS BEAT TIGERS, 4-3 |
| 4TH RED SOX | 82 | 72 | 8 | (YANKEES WON SEASON SERIES, 13-9) |

| 1941 | W | L | GB | WORLD SERIES |
|---|---|---|---|---|
| 1ST YANKEES | 101 | 53 | - | YANKEES BEAT DODGERS, 4-1 |
| 2ND RED SOX | 84 | 70 | 17 | (YANKEES WON SEASON SERIES, 13-9) |

| 1942 | W | L | GB | WORLD SERIES |
|---|---|---|---|---|
| 1ST YANKEES | 103 | 51 | - | YANKEES LOST TO CARDINALS, 4-1 |
| 2ND BOSTON | 93 | 59 | 8 | (RED SOX WON SEASON SERIES, 12-10) |

**1943-44-45**—WAR YEARS

| **1946** | W | L | GB | WORLD SERIES |
|---|---|---|---|---|
| 1ST RED SOX | 104 | 50 | - | RED SOX LOST TO CARDINALS, 4-3. |
| 3RD YANKEES | 87 | 67 | 17 | (RED SOX WON SEASON SERIES, 14-8) |

| **1947** | W | L | GB | WORLD SERIES |
|---|---|---|---|---|
| 1ST YANKEES | 97 | 57 | - | YANKEES BEAT DODGERS, 4-3. |
| 3RD RED SOX | 83 | 71 | 14 | (YANKEES WON SEASON SERIES, 13-9) |

| **1948** | W | L | GB | WORLD SERIES |
|---|---|---|---|---|
| 2ND RED SOX | 96 | 59 | 1 * | INDIANS BEAT THE BRAVES, 4-2 |
| 3RD YANKEES | 94 | 60 | 2.5 | (RED SOX WON SEASON SERIES, 14-8) |

* RED SOX LOST ONE-GAME PLAYOFF TO INDIANS TO DECIDE AL PENNANT.

| **1949** | W | L | GB | WORLD SERIES |
|---|---|---|---|---|
| 1ST YANKEES | 97 | 57 | - | YANKEES BEAT DODGERS, 4-1 |
| 2ND RED SOX | 96 | 58 | 1 * | (YANKEES WON SEASON SERIES, 13-9) |

* YANKEES BEAT RED SOX IN THE FINAL TWO GAMES OF THE SEASON TO WIN AL.

| **1950** | W | L | GB | WORLD SERIES |
|---|---|---|---|---|
| 1ST YANKEES | 98 | 56 | - | YANKEES BEAT PHILLIES, 4-0. |
| 3RD RED SOX | 94 | 60 | 4 | (YANKEES WON SEASON SERIES, 13-9) |

| **1951** | W | L | GB | WORLD SERIES |
|---|---|---|---|---|
| 1ST YANKEES | 98 | 56 | - | YANKEES BEAT GIANTS, 4-2. |
| 3RD RED SOX | 87 | 67 | 11 | (RED SOX WON SEASON SERIES, 11-10) |

# Joe & Ted: Where They Rank

*A look at baseball's career offensive leaders and where Joe DiMaggio and Ted Williams ranked through the 2009 season:*

## GAMES

| | | |
|---|---|---|
| 1. | PETE ROSE | 3,562 |
| 2. | CARL YASTRZEMSKI | 3,308 |
| 3. | HENRY AARON | 3,298 |
| 4. | RICKEY HENDERSON | 3,081 |
| 5. | TY COBB | 3,035 |
| 104. | TED WILLIAMS | 2,292 |
| 409. | JOE DIMAGGIO | 1,736 |

## AT-BATS

| | | |
|---|---|---|
| 1. | PETE ROSE | 14,053 |
| 2. | HENRY AARON | 12,364 |
| 3. | CARL YASTRZEMSKI | 11,988 |
| 4. | CAL RIPKEN JR. | 11,551 |
| 5. | TY COBB | 11,429 |
| 160. | TED WILLIAMS | 7,706 |
| 289. | JOE DIMAGGIO | 6,821 |

Joe's .325 career batting average ranked 31st on the all-time list through the 2009 season.

## RUNS

| | |
|---|---|
| 1. RICKEY HENDERSON | 2,295 |
| 2. TY COBB | 2,245 |
| 3. BARRY BONDS | 2,227 |
| 4. HENRY AARON | 2,174 |
| BABE RUTH | 2,174 |
| 17. TED WILLIAMS | 1,798 |
| 89. JOE DIMAGGIO | 1,390 |

Ted's final home run came in his last at-bat on Sept. 28, 1960 off Baltimore pitcher Jack Fisher. He concluded his career with 521.

## HITS

| | |
|---|---|
| 1. PETE ROSE | 4,256 |
| 2. TY COBB | 4,191 |
| 3. HENRY AARON | 3,771 |
| 4. STAN MUSIAL | 3,630 |
| 5. TRIS SPEAKER | 3,514 |
| 69. TED WILLIAMS | 2,654 |
| 163. JOE DIMAGGIO | 2,214 |

## DOUBLES

| | |
|---|---|
| 1. TRIS SPEAKER | 792 |
| 2. PETE ROSE | 746 |
| 3. STAN MUSIAL | 725 |
| 4. TY COBB | 723 |
| 5. CRAIG BIGGIO | 668 |
| 35. TED WILLIAMS | 525 |
| 181. JOE DIMAGGIO | 389 |

## TRIPLES

| | |
|---|---|
| 1. SAM CRAWFORD | 309 |
| 2. TY COBB | 297 |
| 3. HONUS WAGNER | 252 |
| 4. JAKE BECKLEY | 243 |
| 5. ROGER CONNOR | 233 |
| 78. JOE DIMAGGIO | 131 |
| 380. TED WILLIAMS | 71 |

## HOME RUNS

| | |
|---|---|
| 1. BARRY BONDS | 762 |
| 2. HENRY AARON | 755 |
| 3. BABE RUTH | 714 |
| 4. WILLIE MAYS | 660 |
| 5. KEN GRIFFEY JR. | 625 |
| 18. TED WILLIAMS | 521 |
| 69. JOE DIMAGGIO | 361 |

## RUNS BATTED IN

| | |
|---|---|
| 1. HENRY AARON | 2,297 |
| 2. BABE RUTH | 2,213 |
| 3. CAP ANSON | 2,076 |
| 4. BARRY BONDS | 1,996 |
| 5. LOU GEHRIG | 1,995 |
| 13. TED WILLIAMS | 1,839 |
| 44. JOE DIMAGGIO | 1,537 |

## BASE ON BALLS

| | |
|---|---|
| 1. BARRY BONDS | 2,558 |
| 2. RICKEY HENDERSON | 2,190 |
| 3. BABE RUTH | 2,062 |
| 4. TED WILLIAMS | 2,021 |
| 5. JOE MORGAN | 1,865 |
| 247. JOE DIMAGGIO | 790 |

## STRIKEOUTS

| | |
|---|---|
| 1. REGGIE JACKSON | 2,597 |
| 2. SAMMY SOSA | 2,306 |
| 3. JIM THOME | 2,298 |
| 4. ANDRES GALA RAGE | 2,003 |
| 5. JOSE CANSECO | 1,942 |
| 485. TED WILLIAMS | 709 |
| 1,364. JOE DIMAGGIO | 369 |

# BATTING AVERAGE

| | |
|---|---|
| 1. TY COBB | .367 |
| 2. ROGERS HORNSBY | .358 |
| 3. ED DELAHANTY | .346 |
| 4. TRIS SPEAKER | 345 |
| 5. BILLY HAMILTON | .344 |
| 5. TED WILLIAMS | .344 |
| 31. JOE DIMAGGIO | .325 |

# About the Author

JOHN VALERINO was born in Lakewood, OH., in 1952, but spent most of his childhood in Windsor, CN., from where he made frequent trips to Fenway Park in Boston. A 1974 graduate of Florida Southern College in Lakeland, FL., John spent 30 years at *The Ledger* in Lakeland, 25 as the newspaper's executive sports editor. He also served as the sports coordinator for *The New York Times* Regional Newspaper Group from 1989-2003. He covered three Olympic Games, Major League Baseball, as well as college football, basketball and baseball. He won numerous state and national journalism awards. A pitcher in high school, he was scouted by several clubs until he developed tendonitis his senior year. He and his wife, Lorraine, have two daughters: Mackenzie and Quinn; a son-in-law, Brandon; and three grandchildren: Jason, Emma and Kaylyn. This book is a product of therapy for an illness John has been fighting to overcome for several years, major clinical depression. He is one of 21 million Americans suffering from the disease.

Rookie Mickey Mantle (center) finds himself flanked in 1951 by two of baseball's greatest players.

# TURNING TWO
## BASEBALL'S CLASSIC KEYSTONE COMBINATIONS

JOHN VALERINO'S first book, *Turning Two: Baseball's Keystone Combinations*, takes a look at baseball's top double-play tandems, the relationship between the second baseman and the shortstop. The Foreword was written by former Yankee all-star second baseman Bobby Richardson and the Introduction was authored by former Tiger all-star shortstop Alan Trammell. It is available through:

mackquinnllc@aol.com
*(for personalized note and signature)*

www.wordassociation.com
www.amazon.com
www.barnesandnoble.com
www.borders.com

WA